W9-ATD-575

ONE MORNING THERE WAS A KNOCKING ON THE DOOR.

When Betty opened it, a woman in a black suit and carrying a note pad stepped inside and stared at the three of us.

"Well, this will never do," she said. She went to her car and returned with three brown cardboard suitcases. Giving one to each of us, she spoke sharply. "I want you to put your clothes in there and be quick about it."

We had never packed anything before—there had never been any reason to. But we stuffed a few of our clothes into the suitcases and buckled the straps. Then the woman ushered us out to her car and we sped away.

We did not look back at the house, and we were too afraid to speak. We did not know that now we were wards of the state—and that we would never see our home again. . . .

THE SUITCASES

ANNE HALL WHITT lived the orphan life described in *The Suitcases*, and her home and family count most with her. She lives with her husband and two sons in Gaithersburg, Maryland.

Thoughtful Reading from SIGNET

(0451)

☐ **CITY KID by Mary MacCracken.** The story of a woman who becomes a "therapeutic tutor" for an apathetic second grader headed toward juvenile delinquency, told with warmth and sincerity. ". . . a halting portrayal of a troubled child and a woman's selfless commitment to young people."—*ALA Booklist*   (126467—$3.50)*

☐ **P.S. YOUR NOT LISTENING by Eleanor Craig.** The compelling story of a teacher's efforts to help five emotionally disturbed children face the real world and survive. "All the time Mrs. Craig is there, listening with the third ear, helping the children to understand, and making us understand too."—*Washington Post Book World.*

(121945—$2.95)

☐ **SIGNALS: What Your Child Is Really Telling You by Paul Ackerman, Ph.D. and Murray Kappelman, M.D.** The authors show parents how to recognize, evaluate, and respond effectively to the real problems behind such childhood signals as temper tantrums, bedwetting, hyperactivity, stuttering, anorexia, shoplifting, promiscuity, and more. Also includes a section on the role of teachers, pediatricians, and mental health professionals in signal detection and treatment. Index.   (121864—$3.95)*

☐ **36 CHILDREN by Herbert Kohl.** A former teacher recalls his two years in a Harlem school; the difficult but highly rewarding work with frightened children and the frustration of dealing with unresponsive school administrators. A wide selection of stories, poetry, and drawings by the children is included. Illustrations.   (120930—$2.95)

*Prices slightly higher in Canada

Buy them at your local bookstore or use this convenient coupon for ordering.

THE NEW AMERICAN LIBRARY, INC.,
P.O. Box 999, Bergenfield, New Jersey 07621

Please send me the books I have checked above. I am enclosing $_____
(please add $1.00 to this order to cover postage and handling). Send check or money order—no cash or C.O.D.'s Prices and numbers are subject to change without notice.

Name_____

Address_____

City _____ State _____ Zip Code _____

Allow 4-6 weeks for delivery.
This offer is subject to withdrawal without notice.

THE SUITCASES

By
Anne Hall Whitt

Foreword by
Charles Kuralt

A SIGNET BOOK
NEW AMERICAN LIBRARY
TIMES MIRROR

NAL BOOKS ARE AVAILABLE AT QUANTITY DISCOUNTS WHEN USED
TO PROMOTE PRODUCTS OR SERVICES. FOR INFORMATION PLEASE
WRITE TO PREMIUM MARKETING DIVISION, THE NEW AMERICAN
LIBRARY, INC., 1633 BROADWAY, NEW YORK, NEW YORK 10019.

COPYRIGHT © 1982 BY Anne W. Thompson

All rights reserved. Except for the inclusion of brief quotations in a review,
no part of this book may be reproduced or utilized in any form or by any
means, electronic or mechanical, including photocopying, recording or by an
information storage and retrieval system, without permission in writing from
the publisher. For information address Acropolis Books Ltd, 2400 Seven-
teenth Street, N.W., Washington, D.C. 20009

SIGNET TRADEMARK REG. U.S. PAT. OFF. AND FOREIGN COUNTRIES
REGISTERED TRADEMARK—MARCA REGISTRADA
HECHO EN CHICAGO, U.S.A.

SIGNET, SIGNET CLASSIC, MENTOR, PLUME, MERIDIAN AND NAL BOOKS
are published by The New American Library, Inc.,
1633 Broadway, New York, New York 10019

FIRST SIGNET PRINTING, DECEMBER, 1983

1 2 3 4 5 6 7 8 9

PRINTED IN THE UNITED STATES OF AMERICA

For Betty, Carolyn, and Mother

FOREWORD

Journalism is not the field for anyone who wants his work to be remembered. Yesterday's newspaper is used to wrap fish or start fires, and television news programs go past, literally at the speed of light, never to be seen again. I got used to this a long time ago. That is why I was so surprised, upon reading Anne Hall Whitt's poignant story, to find that something I wrote as a young reporter for my hometown paper had survived down all these years, and still meant something to somebody.

I was twenty-one years old, a year out of the University of North Carolina, and prowling the streets for *The Charlotte News*. I wrote a daily column called "People." (That was a more original title in 1956 than it is today.) Each day I would seek out some cop or kid or cab driver and tell his story in a few hundred words. I carried a battered Rolleicord camera over my shoulder for taking a picture to go with the column. I felt there was some kind of romance in my job: I was Damon Runyon, recording life in the streets, except that the streets I had to work with were Trade and Tryon rather than Broadway. It didn't matter. I used to walk bravely up to panhandlers and back-alley crap shooters—the sort of people others avoided—and strike up a conversation.

I think Malcolm Whitt was sitting on a bench in the shaded yard of the Presbyterian Church when I first noticed him. The churchyard is right downtown, and on fair days its benches were pretty well occupied by old folks with tired feet, most of them down on their luck and with no place else to go.

He was alone, I'm sure of that. He needed a shave. His crutches, leaning against the bench, called attention to his missing leg. His eyes showed sadness.

Of course I walked right over and sat down. This was twenty-five years ago, but my memory is that he welcomed the company. Before long, he was quoting to me from Shakespeare and Robert Burns in a deep rumbling voice, interrupting himself to point out the philosophical importance of these lines of poetry, carrying on a rich monologue. I took out my notebook and wrote it all down, and that didn't cause him to blink an eye.

I must have sat there for an hour or more with this surprising man. I had left him and gone back to the office to write my column about him before I realized I had learned almost nothing about who he was. He lived in the County Home, he said. His name was Malcolm Whitt. That was all.

I saw him on other days after that, and stopped to have a word with him, hoping he wouldn't start another oration because I always had some place to go. I must have asked him about his past, but I never found out anything.

Until now.

Charles Kuralt
CBS News

PREFACE

The year is 1936, the month is March, the place is Charlotte, North Carolina. Three little sisters—the oldest not yet eight—have just returned from a chill cemetery and the funeral of their mother. Bewildered by all that has happened, they enter their old Victorian house with their grieving father, and the door closes behind them.

When next that door opens for them, the sisters will find themselves swept into the strange, frightening world of the orphan and foster child, a more threatening world than anyone who has not lived in it can know.

The story is told by six-year-old Anne, the rebellious and protective middle sister, who, like the others, does not understand what is being done to them. And the great injustice is that no one tells them.

For 1936, choose any date you wish, for it is happening today. For Charlotte, choose any place that comes to mind. For the three little girls, choose children of any age, singly or in combination.

"In the little world in which children exist," wrote Charles Dickens, "there is nothing so finely perceived and so finely felt as injustice."

This, then, is the true story of three orphaned sisters during the Great Depression in the South, and the injustices done them. It is a story of family, love, loss, and survival. And to the extent that it illustrates the frightened helplessness of the foster child, it is more than my personal narrative.

Anne Hall Whitt

"Children, tossed to and fro,
and carried about with every wind . . ."

Ephesians 4, 14

CHAPTER I

Spring comes slowly to the Blue Ridge. Snows that have covered the peaks and filled the valleys since October stay on, almost into May. Winter is reluctant to leave, and when it does, it is in icy streams that splash and tumble down the mountainsides. But it was spring once more, the snows were gone, dogwood and rhododendron were in bloom.

The ever-changing beauty of these Carolina mountains was something I savored from one season to the next. In the fall they blazed with color, in winter they disappeared in snow. But the spring was special to me, as I again felt the world around me waken from its cold deep sleep.

Now the yellow flowers of the spicebush blended with the red and pink azaleas, growing wild over the hillsides. White blossoms of the great silverbell impregnated the air with their fragrance.

I had spent six years in these hazy blue hills, watching the seasons change, my mind often adrift in the clouds of an adolescent girl. I had watched an Easter morning sunrise from the top of Grandfather Mountain, the sleeping old man. I knew every ridge, every curve in the mountain

11

roads that brought me here each fall from my home in Charlotte, one-hundred-and-fifty miles away in the Piedmont to the east.

But on this spring morning in 1950, as I walked the half-mile path to the village postoffice, I wanted to memorize it all, for this was to be my last spring in these mountains. Tomorrow was my graduation day.

———————

To an outsider, Crossnore might not seem like much. A store, a post office, a theater, a cafe, and a boarding school founded and directed by the most determined woman to ever set foot in these mountains. It was this woman, Dr. Mary Martin Sloop, who had encouraged me to take the two-year business administration course after I finished high school at Crossnore. I could not afford to go to college. Few of the children from her school could manage that. But I wanted something more than high school.

"I could use your help in my office," Mrs. Sloop had said, "and you could stay on for the business course. That way you will have your skills and not be beholden to anyone." I realized that she had thought it all through, and as simply as that my education was decided.

Most of the business courses were taught by Leona Moldenhauer, a small woman with crystal blue eyes and a penchant for perfection. Outside of class she became a valued friend, and I spent many hours in her apartment trying new cake recipes, playing with her young son, and talking. With her support and encouragement, I became a straight-A student and received three awards when I graduated.

A few days before I was to finish the two-year course, Mrs. Sloop had called me into her office. I knew from her expression that she was pleased with what she had to tell me. "What is it?" I asked, trying to be matter of fact, although my voice betrayed my excitement.

"Anne, because of your excellent grades, you have been offered a position in Washington," she said.

Working in her office for the past two years, I had come to know her so well. Now as I sat watching her—the lines crinkling around her eyes, the full mouth that smiled so easily, the white hair that never stayed in place—I knew I would miss her very much. She had passed through my life quickly, in six short years—yet how readily and without rebellion I had accepted her teachings. Seated before her, seeing her mischievous smile, I knew that leaving would not be easy.

The time had come for me to be on my own. For so long I had wondered how and where to begin. Now through Mrs. Sloop, my search for a beginning was given to me, with all her good wishes. I knew that for the whole of my life I could never forget this woman or what she meant to me.

As I entered the post office that spring morning I saw Mr. Dellinger, the postmaster, sorting his mail, and I felt sad knowing I would not come here again. When I think of Mr. Dellinger now it is with a smile. He was a raconteur, full of whimsy, and a tease. He sometimes pretended that I was one of the FBI's ten-most-wanted criminals, whose pictures were on his walls. His ambition was to catch one of them and receive a huge reward.

"Morning, Mr. Dellinger," I called through the small window, from which he conducted his business.

"Well, good morning to you, Anne," he replied, lowering his head to look at me over his glasses. "I guess you've come for your package. It's from Charlotte and it's a big one. Probably a graduation gift from home."

As he talked, he brought the package around to the

door. "Too large to go through the window," he said as he set it down in front of me.

He watched as I struggled to lift the box. "The only way you'll get that back to your dormitory is for me to cut a hole in the box and make a handle for you," he said in the fatherly way he talked to the children from the school. A hole was quickly cut, a handle made, and I hurried out of the post office, trying to imagine what could be in this huge box.

I did not feel like sharing my package with the other girls in the dormitory. When I reached the lake where we ice skated in winter, I ran across the little bridge to the other side and sat on one of the rocks we used for putting on our skates.

Peeking into the hole Mr. Dellinger had made, I saw something large and dark. After much ripping and tearing I was able to get the box opened, and for a moment I simply stared. It was the most beautiful suitcase I had ever seen. I ran my hand over the green leather binding, then saw there was a lock and key. I had never owned anything with a lock and key before. I turned the key two or three times to watch the lock pop open. The suitcase was lined with green taffeta, with pockets all around, and folded neatly inside tissue paper was a pale yellow organdy dress. On top of the tissue was a note.

"Dearest Anne," I read. "How I wish I could be with you for your graduation, but I cannot get away from my teaching at this time. You know I will be thinking of you. I hope you like your gifts. The dress is for your graduation. The suitcase is for your trip to Washington. I am so proud of you. Love, Mother." She always wrote short letters. Each sentence was a complete thought, and she did not elaborate on her thoughts.

Looking at the dress and suitcase, I wanted to laugh and

cry. The laughter came as I thought of this woman who signed her letters "Mother." She had been that to me for the past dozen years, since my sisters and I first came to live with her as orphans. I could imagine her shopping for these gifts, and it was out of love that she had sent me this package. But I had realized long ago that her gifts also had a way of serving a purpose.

The dress, carefully chosen in my favorite color and style, was her way of saying, "Now Anne, it is only proper that you wear this on such an occasion as your graduation." As for the suitcase, she had for all my years at Crossnore been horrified at the way I carried my clothes back and forth on the bus or train to school. A sturdy shopping bag had served me just fine, but it was an embarrassment to Mother. "I do not like suitcases," I had told her the few times she mentioned it.

She did not pursue the subject of the shopping bags, and saved them for me in a corner of the pantry. As I came and went from Crossnore, she always had a supply ready. But her thoughtful looks as I got on the bus with them would confuse me.

Now as I admired this beautiful new suitcase, other recollections swept over me. They were memories best forgotten, I had told myself more than once. "Put them away, it is over."

But it was this new suitcase, sitting in the spring sunshine, surrounded by rhododendron, saying that I should let those memories unroll once more—remember that other suitcase for one last time, then put it out of my thoughts forever.

Memories of a childhood. Where do they begin? Do they ever end?

For me, they began in a big clapboard house on Caldwell Street in downtown Charlotte, North Carolina. There we lived as a family. The Victorian charm of the house, with its crenelated windows and ornate trimmings, was lost in its visible lack of repair.

Once white, the house now was grey. A shutter was missing here and there, and the heavy wooden doors creaked on rusting hinges. The wind slipped through cracks in the siding, and there was a chill even in the three downstairs rooms that were heated. By 1936, the Depression had devastated almost everyone, and I guess we were fortunate to have even that old house.

I liked our house. The rooms were large, with high ceilings and thick wooden moldings. Most of the rooms had fireplaces with ornate mantles. There was a big swing on the front porch, and lots of hiding places in the shrubs beyond. In the summer, bees swarmed around the lilac bush where my sisters and I made mud pies in a little patch of dirt. I can see my mother now as she sat on a stump and pretended to eat the pies, served on a bed of leaves.

My mother was of English ancestry, with brown eyes and auburn hair. There was an almost theatrical beauty in the nearly perfect features of her face and the slow, graceful way that she walked. My memory is that she was soft-spoken, neat, and loving in a quiet way. She was respected in the neighborhood for her reserved nature and for her allegiance to her husband and children. I have fleeting recollections of the way she squinted into the sunlight, how she tilted her head as she brushed her long hair, and I can almost see her now standing on the porch at dusk, calling my sisters and me to come indoors.

My father was a large man whose Scottish ancestry was evident in his sandy, wavy hair, ruddy complexion, and eyes as blue as the sea. He was as gregarious as my mother was quiet, and his laughter was loud and contagious. Sometimes he walked down the main street of Charlotte singing his favorite Scottish or Irish songs. If he met a beggar, he gave him his last dime.

He had no inhibitions about life or his love of it. He took my sisters and me to the park, ran down the big slopes with us, and pushed us in the swings. Saturday mornings he would take us to the movies to see cartoons, then to Woolworth's to buy candy. I loved to ride on his shoulders and hear him sing "Annie Laurie" to me. I think my mother's favorite times were when my father would gather us around him in the quiet of an evening and read Robert Burns poetry to us.

My sister Betty was seven-and-a-half years old, with silver-blonde hair that hung in curls to her shoulders. Her great love was books, and I thought she could read better than anybody. At school she excelled in every subject. People always remarked about her attractive manners and how advanced she was for her age.

Carolyn, who was four, was a miniature of our mother in appearance and in the quiet, gentle way she treated life. Unknowingly, she charmed everyone.

I had just turned six, and about all that could be said for me was that my eyes and mouth were too large and I didn't have a care in the world. Relatives summed me up by saying, "Anne is just like her father." That might have been. I only know that my father was then the most important part of my life.

Living with us, I cannot forget my mother's father. He was a small, frail man and blind, but I never thought of him that way. He taught my sisters and me how to tie our shoes and how to tell time by the big mantle clock. The clock had Roman numerals, and for years we could not tell time by any other kind of clock. On a summer day he liked to take walks to a market near the house. Betty held his hand while Carolyn and I skipped ahead. "Wait when you get to the curb," he would call to us. I liked being with my grandfather, he could kiss away bruises and dry our tears better than anyone.

The grimness of the Depression had little effect on my sisters and me. We did not know that our house was shabby or that our father's career as a civil engineer had been crushed. We thought it was wonderful that he was a city policeman and delighted in wearing his cap with the silver badge.

There were picnics in the park and visits to relatives. Our mother and father loved us, and like other parents, they had dreams for their children.

————————

My mother had been ill for several days, and one morning in early March of 1936, my father called the doctor. Aunt Carrie, my mother's sister and probably the person she was closest to, came to the house. She was a short, thin woman who gave the impression of always being busy. Her speech and movements were quick, although she often smiled and seemed to enjoy our visits to her home. Her only child, Bobby, was close to Betty's age and was a constant playmate of ours. Uncle Charlie, the dominant one in their family, was an agreeable man, but I remember him mostly reading the newspaper and listening to the radio.

When Aunt Carrie came into our house that March morning, she immediately took my sisters and me upstairs. We were seldom allowed to go there, especially during the winter months. We ran through the big empty rooms, then kneeled at the front window to play a game. We each chose a color, and whoever counted the most cars of her color passing the house was the winner. The game was suddenly interrupted when Aunt Carrie came into the room crying.

She held the three of us and said, "Your mother is dead." Maybe because we had never known anyone who had died, or maybe because no one had ever explained death to us, her words had no meaning. My aunt then took us downstairs, and told us we must not do anything to upset our daddy.

Seeing him standing in the doorway with the doctor, I realized that what my aunt told us must be awful. The doctor had his arm around my father and he was saying, "I am sorry, Malcolm, your wife had double pneumonia and there was nothing I could do." My father was crying uncontrollably, and it frightened me. When he saw the three of us, he gathered us up in his arms and wept harder.

The funeral took place on Carolyn's fifth birthday. It was the sort of experience about which adults—with all good intentions—will say, "The children will not remember this." But they are wrong. I will always remember the details of that day—the huge ball lights outside the funeral home, the smell of roses, the color of my mother's dress, and the look on my father's face.

Later I remember standing by the open grave in the churchyard on that chilly, damp morning. Aunt Carrie held her handkerchief over her face as the minister said the final words. My father somehow seemed out of place. His face was grey, his eyes stared far off, his hand was cold. People spoke to him but he did not answer.

My father was an only child and had just two relatives—his bedridden mother and his Aunt Florence. As we walked away from the grave, Aunt Florence put her arm around my father and told him how sorry she was. Then my mother's brothers and sisters came to us with their condolences. Uncle Lester, a tall, reedy man with scary dark eyes, patted my father on the shoulder and walked on. I never saw him again. Aunt Thelma, a plump woman with a beautiful face, held us to her perfumed bosom and cried. Aunt Anne, for whom I was named, kissed the three of us on the forehead without touching us and said, "Poor dears." Aunt Carrie was so distraught that Uncle Charlie left quickly with her.

A few days after the funeral, Aunt Thelma came to our house, put me on her generous lap, and scrubbed my dirty knees. Aunt Anne came to see us once but said we made her nervous, and left soon after for her home in Cleveland. It was to be twenty years before I saw either of these relatives again.

We visited Aunt Carrie several times after my mother's death. She was kind but taciturn in her grief. Because of her strong resemblance to my mother, our visits had a disturbing effect on me. The sound of her voice from another room made me think my mother was there, and I would instinctively turn in that direction. Whatever death was, it could not be forever. In my simple mind I knew that one morning I would wake up and Mother would be there, sweeping the kitchen and telling us to hurry with breakfast so we could go out and play.

It was often said that my father had been spoiled by his doting mother. I liked to visit her. She always wore a pink wooly bedjacket, and her room smelled of the sweet talcum powder she used. I would sit against her pillows with her while she showed me little trinkets she kept in a box. Because I was so like my father, I was her favorite. Once she gave me a doll someone had found in the rain. She had made it a bonnet and cape. But the doll's face was a network of cracks and I hated it. I kept the doll turned face down in a box.

After my mother died, we visited my grandmother a few times. But her attention was focused on my father. With a despairing look he listened and said nothing as she lamented, "Oh, my poor son, my poor son." I am not sure how or when my grandmother died, but I feel certain she left this earth thinking that my mother's death had been unfair to my father.

Once my father took us back to the churchyard to see the tombstone with my mother's name on it—Ada Hall Whitt, 1896–1936. A few times we stood by the big iron gates of the cemetery with him, but we never went inside again.

———————

The days at home were long and lonely. While my father was at work, Grandfather took care of us as best he could. But he did not go for walks anymore and would spend most of the day in bed, sometimes rousing just enough to ask if we were all right or to tell Betty how to keep the fire going. Then one night he too died peacefully in his sleep.

My father stayed lost in his grief—the laughter and songs were gone. It was as if his vision of the future had vanished completely. Each day when he left for work he locked the door and told us not to open it for anybody. Betty was not allowed to go to school. The house seemed enormous now, with every sound from within and without echoing through it. Betty would read to us, but mostly we sat in our rocking chairs by the window and waited for our father to come home. When Carolyn cried, I tried to make her laugh the way I used to. I prided myself on the funny faces I could make, and I could talk like Donald Duck. But she screamed at me to stop.

When my father came home in the evening, he took us to a Wimpy's hamburger stand for dinner. Then we walked until my legs ached. Sometimes we went north on Tryon Street until we reached the end of the main part of town. Other times we walked to the courthouse and sat on the benches, watching people and cars go by. My father never sang anymore or put us on his shoulders—he seemed lost in his own world.

Our days went by in isolation until one morning there was a knock at the door. We sat very still, hoping whoever it was would go away. But the knocking became louder and a woman's voice demanded, "Open this door!" Betty went to see who it was. Betty had become our leader, Carolyn and I looked to her for the answers to everything. After all she was older, she could read, and she was enormously stoic.

When Betty opened the door, a woman in a black suit and carrying a note pad stepped inside and stared at the three of us. "Well, they were right," she said. Then she went from room to room, asking, "Who built this fire?" "Why is there no food in the icebox?" "When was the last time you had a bath?" And looking at Betty, she asked, "Why are you not in school, child?"

As for the fire, Betty built it each morning, carefully laying the papers and placing the logs as our grandfather had taught her. The icebox had been empty since our mother died, but there was peanut butter and crackers for our lunch. The last time we had a real bath was when Aunt Carrie had put the three of us in the tub the morning of the funeral. Betty was embarrassed about not being in school because she loved school so much, but she could not tell this strange woman that her father would not let her go. She never answered the question.

"Well, this will never do," said the woman. She went to her car and returned with three brown cardboard suitcases. Giving one to each of us, she spoke sharply. "I want you to put your clothes in these and be quick about it."

We had never packed anything before—there had never been any reason to. But we stuffed a few of our clothes into the suitcases and buckled the straps. Then the woman ushered us out to her car and we rode away.

We did not look back at the house, and we were too afraid to speak. We did not know that now we were wards of the state—and that we would never see our home again.

CHAPTER II

~~~~~~~~~~~~~~~~~~~~~~~~~~~~~~

Turning down a narrow street on the other side of town, the woman in black stopped the car in front of a large stone building with the words "The Catholic Home" carved above the door. "Come on, girls, get your suitcases and hurry along," she said as she guided us out of the car and up the steps.

The foyer was dimly lit and smelled of candles and tomato soup. In a corner was a small statue on a pedestal and above it a gold cross. We trailed behind the woman in black down a narrow hallway, passing an empty dining room and what looked like a classroom. I could hear the muffled voices of children upstairs.

She led us into an office where a large nun sat facing away from us behind a heavy table that served as a desk. "Well, Sister Catherine," said the woman in black, "I have brought you three more." She started her sentences with "Well," as if all were hopeless.

When Sister Catherine turned to us, I saw a not-unkind face, with the weary look of one who must give orders and would rather not. She stood up and came around the side of the desk toward us.

The woman in black said things to her like "improper care," "no food in the house," "their mother dead," and "the oldest one not in school." Sister Catherine came nearer. I had never seen a nun up close before, and the enormity of her being and her habit frightened me.

"Pity," she said, looking down at us. Then to the woman in black she said, "As you know, we are overcrowded here, and with the Depression, we are as poor as everyone else. We will not be able to keep them too long, but they may stay until you can make other arrangements." The woman thanked her and left, promising to find another place as soon as possible.

While Sister Catherine studied the folders left by the woman in black, my sisters and I sat on a hard wooden bench along the wall, with the suitcases on the floor in front of us. "The first thing we must do is see what clothing you brought with you," she said as much to herself as to us. We put the suitcases up on the table and watched as she examined the contents of each one. "Not a single matching sock, no sweaters, no nightclothes," she sighed. Then she tapped a small bell on her desk, and a frail nun with faded blue eyes entered the room. "These three little girls are sisters—would you see that they get settled before dinner?"

Without speaking, the nun led us up a dark stairway and into a bathroom at the end of the hall. Running a tub of water, she told us to undress. A bare light bulb swinging overhead made strange shadows on the pale green walls and worn linoleum floor. The room and the house were quiet except for the occasional sound of a child's voice. I saw the bewildered looks on Betty's and Carolyn's faces, and felt my body tense.

With a brush and a large bar of strong-smelling soap, the nun scrubbed us from the top of our heads to the soles of our feet. As she dug into my skin and scalp, she mumbled. "Why must I do this when my back aches so? Never saw such dirty children. If only I could lie down for awhile." I was sorry for her, but already felt a dislike.

Then wearing the strange dark dresses with white aprons that we had been given, we were taken into a big room with many beds. On each bed sat a little girl dressed as we were, and under each bed was a suitcase just like ours. The nun told us to sit quietly on our new beds with our suitcases underneath and wait for dinner.

After she left, I whispered to Betty, "Where are we?"

"I don't know."

Carolyn sat close to Betty, her brown eyes expressing the fear that each of us felt.

This was the first time we had been with other children since our mother died, and I suddenly had the urge to play hide and seek. I offered to be "It," and soon the room was filled with giggling little girls, hiding under beds and behind doors.

The fun ended abruptly when the nun who had bathed us returned and clapped her hands loudly. After a lecture on obeying the rules and strict punishment if we didn't, she ordered us to line up for the dining room.

In the dining room I was surprised to see as many boys as there were girls. There were infants and teenagers. A nun with heavy eyebrows stood at the head of our table, and we all remained standing while Sister Catherine said grace.

Seated next to me at the long plain table was a small boy with black hair and freckles. He ate only a few mouthfuls of his dinner, then began to cry. A plump girl on the other side of the table leaned across and chanted, "Billy is a cry-baby!" I asked her why he was crying. "Oh, he cries all the time," she said. "He doesn't have any family, and he'll probably be here forever."

How sad, I thought. I had a father and two sisters, and I knew my father would soon come and get us.

As we got into bed that night, I whispered to Betty, "Daddy is not going to like it when he comes home and finds us gone."

"I know."

"Will he come and get us tomorrow?"

"I'm sure he will."

For a while I lay on the strange narrow cot, thinking about my daddy alone in our big house. I thought about the woman in black who had brought us here, and wondered who she was. Carolyn had cried until Betty lay down beside her, then both had fallen asleep. I also went to sleep, certain that wherever we were, my father would find us and take us home.

The next day we were awakened by the mysterious sounds of the nuns at morning mass. "Hail Mary, full of grace," they recited in unison. For a moment I was calmed by the soft rise and fall of their voices, but still I took little comfort in remembering that my mother had told me that nuns, dressed in black, were doing God's work on Earth.

When a nun came to gather us for breakfast, I went up to her and asked, "Will my daddy be here today?"

"I do not know, child," she said. "Are you expecting him?"

"Oh, yes," I replied, "He'll be coming to take us home."

She looked at me. "Hurry or you will be late for morning prayers."

After prayers and breakfast, the three of us were baptized in the chapel—a ritual I found both scary and fascinating. I liked the soft voice of the priest, and there were candles on the altar. But it all reminded me of my mother's funeral, and I could not help wondering what they were going to do to us.

With a white surplice over his cassock, the priest began in a low rhythmic voice, saying words in another language. Then dipping a small silver shell into a bowl of water, he dribbled water slowly over each of our heads as he continued with the rhythm of the words. After he put oil on our foreheads, Sister Catherine told us to kneel, and she prayed for us.

The baptism over, we were allowed to go outside and play. The area behind the Home was enclosed by a high wire fence. There were huge trees, a bit of worn grass, and in a far corner a line of trash cans. Children were playing on swings and slides; most of the boys were playing ball. I had always liked slides, and for a while was distracted by the excitement of sailing off the end of the slide into a pile of sand.

I was at the top of the highest slide when I saw my father coming toward me down the street. Calling to my sisters who were playing nearby, I shouted, "Daddy, Daddy, I knew you would come." I climbed on top of a trash can, from there made my way to the top of the wire fence, and was ready to jump down into my father's arms when a nun came running, calling me by name.

"Get down from there this minute!" she shouted.

But I had already climbed down the other side and was not frightened of the nun and her reprimands. My father was here. He would take us home. I was happy.

The nun hurried through the gate, and in an angry voice told my father, "If you had cared for these children properly, they would not be here." I cannot forget the look in his eyes as he held me close and said nothing.

The nun continued. "You must leave here at once and not bother them anymore."

My father took my arms from around his neck, set me on the ground, and said in a defeated voice, "Go with her, Anne, and be a good girl."

"Will you come back, Daddy?"

"Soon," he said, then turned and walked away. Seeing him so all alone made me very sad.

Betty and Carolyn had come up to the fence, and they watched him walk back down the street.

The nun marched us into the building. "You are never to try leaving these grounds again," she said. "If you do, you will be severely punished." Before she dismissed us, she shook her finger in my face and said, "Do you understand what I am saying to you, child?"

I did not answer, but when she left I realized my teeth were clamped hard together and my fists were clenched. I was shocked at this new emotion raging in me, and was not at all sure what to do with it. As I ran up the stairs, with Betty and Carolyn close behind, I thought I would explode. Seeing my suitcase, I kicked it as hard as I could. "Everything is going to be all right, Anne," said Betty. "We'll go home soon, just like Daddy told you." Carolyn looked at us in confusion.

Before that day ended I had my first fight. I did not like the plump girl who had chanted at the crying boy in the dining room. The girl began to tease Carolyn because she always held Betty's hand and never left her side. I was pulling the girl's hair when a nun came up, separated us, and took me into the chapel. "Now you must stay for a while here and ask forgiveness for your sins," she said.

The only prayer I knew was, "Now I lay me down to sleep. . ." and I had no idea what *sins* meant. But I sat in the chapel for a long time and thought about what was happening to us, and wished that someone would explain.

As the days went by, I became familiar with the chapel. More and more I found myself angry and unable to control my temper. Each time I was told to pray for my sins. My knees hurt as I knelt on the worn velvet pads, but somehow I found solace there as I memorized every detail in the stained glass windows or stared into the face of the man on the cross.

Carolyn became even more withdrawn, and soon refused to eat. Betty worried about her, and returned from dinner one night with her apron pockets full of food. When the lights went out for the night, she fed Carolyn. In the mornings she would fill her pockets with oatmeal, carry a spoon under her apron so as not to get caught, and carefully feed Carolyn before she left for school a block away.

Carolyn looked forward to her private meals with Betty until one morning, as Betty was spooning the oatmeal into Carolyn's mouth, a nun came in. "What is going on here?" she demanded. Standing very tall, her pockets sagging with the oatmeal, Betty looked at the nun. "I am feeding my sister," she said.

Moving closer to Carolyn, the nun said, "Young lady, you must take your meals in the dining room like all the rest of the children." Then she hurried Betty off to wash her apron. Before she left for school, Betty had to go to the chapel to pray. Seeing Betty carrying her soiled apron, her yellow curls bobbing against her shoulders and her eyes that never showed anger, I felt my throat tighten and my fingernails dig into my palms.

While Betty was at school, Carolyn and I sat at the top of the slide and watched for our father. Our legs became numb from the cold steel slide, but we did not give up our vigil. We could also see Betty's school and trains going over a bridge. I remembered the time my father had let us each put a penny on the railroad track when President Roosevelt's train came through town. He said we could keep the penny as a remembrance of the day we had waved to the President. I wondered about the penny. Was it in my room with my other things? I missed the big house, my dolls, and my mother and father.

My reverie was broken by the sound of the lunch bell. I knew that afterwards Carolyn and I would resume our perch, waiting for Betty and our father.

There were times when I felt that I would suffocate within the walls of this place. The urge to run, laugh out loud, and shout was always with me, and to hold back was not easy. If I raised my voice above a whisper, a nun would appear, place her finger against my lips and say, "Practice silence, my child."

Once when I thought I was alone, I slid down the heavy wooden bannister in the hall. At the foot of the stairs stood Sister Catherine, who made me tiptoe up and down the stairs ten times, then placed me on a little stool in the corner of her office.

There may have been no more than a dozen nuns in the Home, but they seemed to surround me, appearing almost magically. They were faces without bodies, forms gliding through shadowy rooms, with only the faint rattle of their beads to announce their passing.

The chapel doors were always open, and I often stood just outside. Sometimes the nuns would be there in a group, reading or silently meditating. Because their services were so foreign to me, they held great fascination, so much so that I was more than once punished for my curiosity. I had gone into the chapel alone and dipped my fingers into the cold holy water to practice crossing myself.

When I did this with the other children at morning mass, I might forget to touch my forehead or my shoulders, and Sister Catherine would scold me afterwards. So alone I practiced the ritual several times. Then I walked down the aisle, knelt briefly as I had seen the nuns do, and was about to turn and leave when a hand was laid on my shoulder and I was guided into a pew. There I spent the rest of the morning.

The priest made daily visits to the Home, but his stay was usually short. One evening he appeared in a long cape with a high collar trimmed in gold. I could not take my eyes off him as we filed into the chapel. The nuns standing in the front pews hid my view of the altar with its flickering candles. Careful to make no sound, I edged sideways to the aisle and watched the priest lift a shiny golden globe which he gently swung above and around the altar. Strange perfumy smoke came from the globe, and its scent filled the chapel. The nuns joined the priest in singing a rhythmic hymn in their strange language. The smell of the smoke made me slightly dizzy, and I was glad that this call to chapel ended quickly.

After breakfast one Saturday, I asked a nun if we could go to the movies. I could smell the starch in her big white collar and see the veins in her face as she bent toward me. "What a ridiculous question. Be grateful you have a roof over your head and food in your stomach." Her answers always had an unsettling effect on me and caused my fears to increase.

As each day ended, I built my hopes for the next day—surely then my father would come to get us. But days turned into weeks and my frustration turned to anger. A display of temper always got the nuns' attention. Maybe if I caused them enough trouble, I reasoned, they would send me back to my father. But I learned that I was not to be rewarded for misbehavior. Whether the nuns used it as catharsis or as punishment I do not know, but I spent long hours learning the Baltimore catechism. Sitting on a stool in front of Sister Catherine, she would ask me, "Who made you?"

"God made me," I would answer, and Sister Catherine gave me a gentle smile.

———————————

One sunny afternoon near the middle of May, my sisters and I were playing hopscotch in the yard when a nun came looking for us: "Sister Catherine wants you children to come to her office."

There we found the woman in black with Sister Catherine. "You are leaving here today, girls," the woman told us. "Get your suitcases quickly."

We hurried up the stairs, pulled the suitcases from under the beds, and hurried back to the office.

When we returned with the suitcases, our mismatched clothes still in them, Sister Catherine looked at us for a long time, then did a strange thing. She placed her hand lightly on each of our heads, touched the heavy silver cross that she wore around her neck, and in a barely audible voice said, "Dear Lord, please let no harm come to these children." She said goodbye to each of us. And as we got to the door, she called out, "Anne, do see if you can stop your fighting. It will get you nowhere in this life."

We walked out into the sunlight wearing our dark dresses and aprons and got into the car with the woman in black. We rode away in silence with our suitcases at our feet.

Our stay at the Catholic Home had been short—scarcely

two months—but for a child the routine, familiar faces, and discipline had supplied security, if not love and affection.

Riding through the streets of Charlotte and watching for landmarks of home, I thought about the children I had left behind, about Sister Catherine whose eyes seemed to penetrate to the depths of everything she saw, and of the little nun who had to chase me every day for a bath.

There was a lump in my throat, but I swallowed hard and thought of going back to live with my father. How happy he would be to see us.

CHAPTER III

The car stopped in front of a large building I had seen on one of my longer walks with our father. I asked Betty what the words said above the door. "Public Health Clinic," she answered.

Leaving the three suitcases in the car, the woman in black took us inside. We sat on a bench in a long hallway that smelled of rubbing alcohol and disinfectants, and watched doctors and nurses come and go, wondering why we were there. After a long wait, we were called one by one into a small room where we were weighed, measured, and vaccinated. Unprepared for this, I let go with a scream. The woman in black looked in, and said with some satisfaction, "Anne, you are every bit as bad as they told me you were." Then we climbed back into the car, clutching our arms.

The ride from the clinic to the next stop was short. The car turned into a drive that curved under big oak trees and stopped in front of the largest of several brick buildings. Children, tricycles, skates, and balls were everywhere. And there was no fence, only scraggy boxwood shrubs that outlined the grounds.

As we got out of the car, children ran up to greet us. One little girl grabbed my hand. "Do you go to school?" she asked. Before I could reply the woman in black pulled us along, saying, "Hurry up, girls. I haven't much time." Carolyn clung to Betty, dragging her suitcase along by its strap. I glanced at Betty and saw the confident look that told me everything would be all right.

The entrance way to this new place was very different from the Catholic Home. On the wall was a large bulletin board filled with children's drawings. The halls were painted light green. There were no candles. Somebody was playing a piano, somebody was singing, and children—big children, little children, and babies—were everywhere.

We followed the woman in black into a cluttered office. At the desk sat a stout woman in a lavender flowered dress. Looking over her glasses, she greeted the woman in black as if she had known her a long time. Glancing at us, she said to no one in particular, "Three of them, eh?"

"You know," she continued, "we cannot keep them too long here at the orphanage." Then she asked, "What about adoption? What about foster care?" All I understood from their conversation was that this was something called an "orphanage."

The lady in lavender studied the folder of notes given to her by the woman in black. Then she got up and came toward us, asking which one of us was which. For a moment I thought that she was going to smile, but the beginnings of the smile turned into concern as she got a good look at us. "They don't appear too healthy, do they? The report makes no mention of illness—have you girls been sick lately?" she asked, looking at Betty.

"No ma'am," Betty said politely, "only Anne has a lot of sore throats."

"Oh, they'll be all right," said the woman in black, "just

a bit thin maybe." Then she picked up her notebook and said she had to leave.

I was relieved when one of the older children was summoned to the office to take us and our suitcases upstairs. The visit to the health clinic had left me drained, and I felt I could not bear the scrutiny of this orphanage lady for another minute. Her manner toward us was pleasant but businesslike.

Upstairs was a huge room with many beds, and again under each bed was a suitcase identical to ours. The room looked as if someone had tried to make it cheerful, with ruffled curtains at the windows and pictures on the walls.

We were putting our suitcases under our beds when a grey-haired woman came into the room. "The oldest one will have to come with me," she said. Carolyn was not going to let Betty go without her and started to follow, but the grey-haired woman told Carolyn she would have to stay with me. The children who went to school lived in different cottages, and since neither Carolyn nor I attended school, we would remain here.

Until that moment, Carolyn had been content as long as Betty was with her. Now her world collapsed. Looking at her on the bed crying, her brown eyes already showing dark circles under them, and wearing a dress two sizes too large, I felt anger and hatred. But I did not know whom I should be hating. I lay down beside Carolyn, patted her tangled curls, and told her not to cry, that we would see Betty at mealtime and after school.

The routine here was much as it had been at the Catholic Home, but in a more sociable way. The high-pitched voice of the lady in lavender could be heard over the voices of the children, but she did not require that we whisper, as the nuns had. And there was no emphasis on religion, except for Sunday morning services in a tiny brick chapel under big willow oaks behind the orphanage. We quickly fell into this new order of life.

———————

Not long after we arrived, I bumped into a boy as I was coming out of the dining room. He turned, swung at me and said, "Look out, twirp." But he did not look at all angry and his gesture was not hostile. His dark eyes and long lashes were almost hidden by a blue wool cap with a bill pulled down low over his forehead. His corduroy knickers squeaked when he walked, and every other step was a sort of skip. As he passed the lady in lavender, she said, "Hello, Tom." He gave a wave and continued on in his walk, skip fashion with a nonchalant whistle. I decided I liked him.

The next day I followed Tom around until he spoke to me. "Hey, twerp, want to go through the trash with me?"

"What for?" I asked.

"See if I can find some Post Toasties boxes—I want to tear off the tops and send for a Dick Tracy badge."

While Tom searched for the cereal boxes, I looked at discarded magazines. "Oh, look," I said. "Isn't she beautiful?"

Hardly glancing at the magazine picture I pointed to, he said, "Just a dumb old doll."

"Read what it says her name is," I pleaded.

Looking a little closer, he spelled out "*S-o-n-j-a H-e-n-i-e*." "That's a funny name," he said, a little embarrassed that he couldn't pronounce it.

"Who's she?" I asked.

"I dunno," he said, without the slightest interest.

The cook came and told us to get away from the trash. She was short, fat, and playful. In the dining room I had seen her help feed some of the younger children, and she never scolded us for spilling food. She liked to play the old piano in the dining room, picking out the tunes in her own fashion and never using the pedals. She and her husband, the handyman, lived at the orphanage. When I showed her the Sonja Henie doll picture, she said, "That's nice, but who could afford something like that?" Then she told Tom she would save the box tops for him, and sent us to play.

Slowly I began to like the place, which I found out was called the Thompson Orphanage. There were toys, games outdoors after dinner, and there was laughter. There was a nursery full of babies, and there were cottages with older children. Betty was happy to be in school. She had books to read, she could add and subtract, and do all sorts of wonderful things.

Some of my old ebullience returned, and I began turning situations into fun. I could do imitations of the lady in lavender—she waddled when she walked and chewed her bottom lip when one of the children told her about a problem. I could imitate Betty Boop and Popeye, and the horrible faces I made would cause the toughest child in the orphanage to flee in make-believe fright. But there were still times when one of the children threw a rock, took a swing away from me, or bothered Carolyn—Betty had told me never to let her out of my sight—that I got into fights.

The grey-haired woman who had taken Betty to her cottage that first day supervised most of our activities. It did not rankle her if someone's socks didn't match or if our elbows weren't clean, but she detested fighting. She would call out in a sqeaky voice, "You children must love each other!"

Her way of punishing was to make us sit on a stool in

the corner of a small room. I spent a fair amount of time in that little room. Occasionally she would forget she had put me there, and my absence wouldn't be discovered until dinner time. Carolyn would tell Betty about my fighting, and Betty would be furious with me. If only I could have endured as she did, but I could not.

We had been at the orphanage only a couple weeks when we noticed that frequently a child would be called into the office, and a short time later would disappear. And almost every day new children arrived. I was confused by this coming and going of children, and I began to sense the uncertainty of our lives.

"Do you suppose Daddy knows where we are?" I asked Betty one afternoon. "He might think we are still with Sister Catherine."

"He will find us," Betty reassured me.

There was one little girl that I liked. She was tall and skinny, but pretty and very nice, and she was the only person I knew who could climb to the top of the jungle gym and stand up without holding on. One night she came to dinner very excited. "Guess what?" she said. "I'm going to be adopted." When I asked her what that meant, she said, "I am going to live in a real house and have a new mother and daddy." I asked her who made her do this. "Oh, the lady in the office wants to find homes for all of us," she explained.

I did not want a new mother and daddy. Also, I began to wonder what would happen if they took my sisters and didn't take me. This fear haunted me day and night, and when I told my sisters about adoption, we decided we would not leave unless our father came for us. But we knew at the same time this was not possible. If the woman in black came for us, we would go with her just as we had before.

Our dread that we would be separated increased as we watched other children leave. We discovered that when a child left, her suitcase disappeared from under her bed. So if I could not find either of my sisters, I would run to her bed to check if the suitcase was gone. And each day Carolyn and I went to Betty's cottage over and over again to make sure her suitcase was still under her bed.

My suitcase had become my treasure chest. I put in it things I wanted to keep forever: two celluloid soap holders I found in the trash during one of my rummages with Tom, the picture of the Sonja Henie doll, and two large walnuts I had found at the Catholic Home. The outer shell of the walnuts had come off and stained my clothes, but I didn't care. The lady who did the laundry was always scolding me for being dirty, so she took little notice of the dark stains.

It is strange now, thinking back, that the three of us never talked about the future. We could not look forward to summers as children do—we did not talk about tomorrow or even next week. Each day was suspended alone in time. But we talked often about our mother and father, and I sometimes dreamed I was running in the park with him. Other times I thought I heard him singing "Annie Laurie" and at those times I felt my father was somehow really there with me.

The lady in lavender called all of the children together one evening before bedtime, to tell us that the next day was the Fourth of July. One of the women's clubs of Charlotte was sponsoring a picnic for orphans, and in the morning a bus would take us to Myers Park.

Excursions were rare at the orphanage, and the idea of riding a bus to the other side of town was like opening gates for wild horses. In the Catholic Home and the orphanage there had been no reminders of our past. But Myers Park was a place we had been many times with our mother and father, and I could not share in the excitement of the other children. Suddenly I did not want to go.

When the bus unloaded that next day, my sisters and I looked out over the rolling green hills of the park. I thought of the stories my father told of how I had taken my first steps here—never having walked before, I had spent a Sunday afternoon running down those hills. Tears came as I remembered my father with the hat he called his "boater" tilted back on his head, swinging his arms in his carefree manner while my mother walked beside him carrying our picnic basket.

"Come on, girls, you must stay with the group," said the lady in lavender, guiding my sisters and me along. Betty was startled at this interruption of her thoughts and walked away as if in a trance, holding tight to Carolyn's hand.

The children from the orphanage obediently sat at the tables assigned to them while the club ladies gave us hot dogs, potato salad, lemonade, and an American flag. The ladies had brought their families, and soon the park was filled with other people from around the city. It was all very festive, with a band playing "Yankee Doodle" and Sousa marches.

After eating, we were told to stay in that area and play tag. A girl—a prissy little thing in a striped sunsuit, pink ribbons in her curls, came over to me and asked, "What's it like living in an orphanage?" I gave her my best cross-eyed face, and she ran screaming to her mother.

"Mommie, mommie, she's mean!" the girl wailed, pointing to me.

Her mother gave me a glance. "I would stay away from her, dear," she said.

As I watched the mother and daughter turn away, an unfamiliar, uncomfortable feeling of humiliation came over me. I did not know then that orphans evoke feelings of disgust as well as pity in others.

After the club ladies had photographed us in front of our bus and we said a proper thank-you, it was a relief to return to our orphanage.

———————

The summer passed with little to alter the routine of the days. We learned to make our beds, set the table, and take care of anyone smaller than ourselves. Tom and I continued to plunder the trash when the cook was not around. And with some reluctance because I was a girl, Tom let me shoot marbles with him. His three marbles were his only possessions. Putting one of them in the circle drawn with his finger in the dirt, we would take turns trying to shoot it out with the other two marbles. I got to be as good as he, but he never let me keep a marble.

Sometimes I wandered into the garden that was tended by the older children. I liked to pull the carrots and pick the big ripe tomatoes. It was a carefree and not unpleasant life, but I was restless. I could hear the world on the other side of the boxwoods, and sometimes I crawled between them and watched the cars go by. Children stared out of car windows—grownups smiled and waved. But I was lost in the ever-present hope that my father would come for us soon.

School was about to start when the woman in black appeared. Our suitcases were left under the beds, and without explanation we were again driven to the public health clinic. After the examinations were over, I was called back into the doctor's office, where he told the woman my tonsils were bad and would have to come out. "We will get the adenoids too, while we're at it," said the doctor. She did not seem pleased about this, and I wondered what they were talking about.

A few weeks later, I was awakened earlier than the other children, given no breakfast, and told to go with the woman in black to the hospital. She left me with a nurse who dressed me in a gown and sat me in the hall. "Stay on that bench and wait your turn," she said as she left.

I watched people being wheeled past me on long tables. They appeared to be asleep and had tubes coming out of their noses. I was scared. I lay down on the bench and buried my face in my hands to blot out the sights around me and the sickening smell of ether. Was this my punishment for all the bad things I had done since they took me away from my father? I wondered. What would Betty and Carolyn think when they found me gone? If only there were someone to answer all the questions that I had.

Soon a long white table was rolled in. A young man lifted me gently onto the table, covered me with a blanket, and wheeled me into a brightly lighted room. There a black rubber mask was placed over my nose and mouth, and I lost consciousness.

When I woke, I was in a different room, and sitting by my bed was my father. I was sure that I was dreaming because I did not know how I had gotten into this strange room or where my father had come from. He was smiling, and in his hand was a red balloon. In a small brown bag he had two oranges. Sitting up to hug him, I became very ill, and my throat ached—but I had never been happier.

My father explained to me about tonsils and adenoids and said I would be feeling better soon. For the rest of the day he sat by my bed and talked. Times had been difficult, he said, but soon we could all be together again. Then he softly sang "Annie Laurie" to me and I fell asleep. He was gone when I woke up. I ate one of the oranges, though it hurt my throat, and I waited for him to return, but he never did. Back at the orphanage, I put the deflated red balloon in my suitcase, remembered his promise and smiled.

In September—at the age of six-and-a-half—I was enrolled in the first grade at the same school, two blocks from the orphanage, that Betty attended.

Betty very proudly, and with some trepidation, introduced me to my first-grade teacher. "If your sister does as well as you, Betty, I am very glad to have her in my class," said the teacher smiling. This was the last time she was to smile at me.

I liked to read and print the letters of the alphabet. Betty had already taught me how to do this, so I finished long before the others and amused myself by drawing faces in all the letters. Making me do my printing over again, the teacher said, "Why can't you do your work as nicely as your sister?" When an assignment was put on the board, I was kept after school because I did not turn in a paper. "Why do you just sit there, stubbornly refusing to do your work?" the teacher wanted to know.

"I can't see the board," I told her. She seemed pleased at this discovery, and ordered an eye examination. A week later I came to school with new wire-frame glasses. I did the work from the board, but continued to turn in what she called "messy" papers.

Tom and I were watching squirrels gather acorns one October afternoon when a small truck drove up with about a dozen pumpkins. "This happens every year," said Tom in that lighthearted way he had. "Tonight we'll make them into jack o'lanterns."

That night I lost all sense of where I was. I joined in the carving of the pumpkins and will always remember how ghostly they looked Halloween night after the cook's husband placed them along the curved driveway. The cook had painted our faces with crayons, and women from one of the churches brought us black eye masks, tin horns, crickets, and clappers. We marched around making all sorts of noises while the flickering light from the pumpkins cast shadows around us.

Later, while we ate candy corn inside, Tom and I noticed a fur piece one of the women had left on a chair. It was reddish brown, with a small fox's head on one end. The eyes were glassy, and if you pressed on the mouth it opened and closed. I stroked the fur while Tom worked the mouth, until a stout lady with deep waves of grey hair hurried over, rescued her fur and said, "Oh, no, children, you must not touch."

Tom giggled when I stuck out my tongue. "Oh, my goodness!" said the lady as she hurried away.

Winter came. The woman in black took my sisters and me to a sort of warehouse in town, where there was a large room filled with clothing and shoes. My eyes burned from the strong smell of sizing. The clothes were made of the cheapest fabric by women prisoners, and I was fitted into a scratchy, brown wool coat with sleeves that came down over my hands. The shoes were brown lace-ups, and they hurt my feet for weeks. The underwear was cream-colored, heavy, with buttons up the front and across the back which could be undone for going to the bathroom.

The legs came to the knees, the sleeves to the wrist. I disliked this suit—not for its looks, but for the bothersome business of getting in and out of it. The dresses were all of solid-colored shiny material. There were no ruffles, gathers, or sashes—just plain, straight dresses with a single button at the neck.

The children from the orphanage went to the public school, and it was impossible not to notice how other children stared at our clothes. Some would say, "Why do you wear such dresses?" or "Why is your coat so big?" Betty pretended not to notice, but I found their cruelty unbearable and would lunge at them, pulling hair, kicking and hitting. Then I would be punished for "hurting someone." Seeing the other little girls with pastel dresses with smocking or lace trim and their shoes with buckles made me long for pretty clothes.

In the dining room one evening, the lady in lavender rang her bell to get our attention. "Christmas is one week away," she announced. "One of the churches will be bringing us a tree tomorrow, and we will put it right here in the dining room."

"Will Santa Claus come?" asked a child.

"Oh, yes, he will be here on Christmas morning."

The tree arrived, and it was beautiful. We made decorations out of colored paper and cut pictures of Santa out of magazines and pasted them on the windows. The older girls made cookies and iced them in green and red. We sang Christmas carols while the cook played the piano. The night before Christmas we were each told to leave a stocking at our place at the table for Santa to fill.

Christmas Day came, and entering the dining room I thought it was the most beautiful sight I had ever seen. The tree glowed in the morning sunlight, and the assortment of designs we had made and hung on the tree twinkled. A white paper angel had been placed on top, and underneath were many presents. Around the tree were freshly painted bicycles, tricycles, and wagons donated by charitable organizations. These were to be shared by all the children.

Standing in front of the tree was Santa, and I shivered with anticipation. "How could he possibly know what I wanted for Christmas?" I thought. The picture of the Sonja Henie doll was in my suitcase, and I had so hoped to show it to him before today. My mother and father had always taken us to see Santa, and he had come down the chimney, bringing me what I had asked for. But this place was different. There were too many children, I supposed.

We found our filled stockings at our places at the table. In each one was a toothbrush, washcloth, and comb. Not at all what I expected, and certainly not what I would have asked for.

After breakfast, Santa began calling each child to come up and get a gift. Mine was wrapped in white tissue paper with a green ribbon around it. Opening it I found a doll. She was ludicrous. Her flaming red-yarn hair hung down her back, the black button eyes, and red embroidered mouth were sewn on a pink face. Her dress was blue, and she had no shoes or underclothes. Her long arms and legs dangled loosely from her body. I loved her on sight, and named her Emily. I pulled her hair back, tied it with the green ribbon from the package, and cuddled her.

Betty and Carolyn received similar dolls, and with them we began a game we called "play house." We pretended that we were mothers, that the dolls had a daddy, and that we lived in a big, big house.

Ten days after Christmas we were told to be ready to leave the orphanage. On that morning as we packed, I placed

Emily in the bottom of my suitcase, for fear that if I carried her out in my arms they would make me leave her behind. I wanted to go to the playground and swing one last time, and to the kitchen to say goodbye to the cook. I wanted to see Tom, but there was no time. The woman in black was waiting. In the office I heard her say, "Well, I have finally found a place that will take all three of them." I wondered if this would be a home with a new mother and daddy as the skinny girl had said.

Looking very dignified and in a grown-up voice, Betty asked, "Are we going to be adopted?"

"Heavens no," the woman in black replied. "I doubt we'll ever find anybody who will adopt three at once."

The lady in lavender walked to the front door with us. Kneeling down, she buttoned our coats. "You will be all right," she said.

It was the first time I had looked closely at her, and I was surprised at how tired she appeared. I would miss her loud voice and her reprimands shouted from the office window as we played outdoors.

As we drove away, I turned for one last look at the Thompson Orphanage, which had been our home for most of the year. Then the car rounded a curve in the drive and the chapel disappeared in the trees.

It was here that I had come to understand that my mother was gone forever, when the minister at one of the chapel services had said that "to die" meant going to Heaven to live with the angels. This my sisters and I accepted.

CHAPTER IV

~~~~~~~~~~~~~~~~~~~~~~~~~~

The ride was long. The city of Charlotte soon lay behind us, and the openness of the countryside interested me. Houses were set far back off the road, cows grazed on the hillsides, and there was quiet everywhere. Carolyn fell asleep, and Betty and I occasionally whispered to each other.

The winter sun was almost setting when the car turned into a dirt road. In the distance I could see only a small, white, frame house with smoke coming out of the chimney. "That must be it," said the woman as she headed the car toward the house.

We got out of the car holding our suitcases. I looked around and saw chickens, horses, and some cows. There were several small poorly constructed sheds and a barn. A pickup truck, a black car, and a big yellow bus were parked near the house. This was very different from the Catholic Home and the orphanage, and I wasn't sure I was going to like it.

An old lady came to the door and called out, "Thought you folks had gotten lost." Her hair was pulled back in a bun, her glasses were set far down on her nose, and she wore a long dark dress with an apron over it.

Leading us into a small, sparsely furnished room, she said, "Have a seat." The room was cold, the horsehair sofa scratched my legs. The woman in black remained standing and stayed just long enough to say she would be checking on us soon. She seemed relieved to leave.

The old lady looked at us carefully and said, "My name is Mrs. Stamens, but you might as well call me Ma, everybody else does." Then she took us back into the kitchen where it was warm and smelled of coffee and burning wood. A man was sitting by a big black stove, warming his hands. "This here is my husband, and you can call him Pa," she said.

Mr. Stamens leaned forward in his chair, spat something brown into a can and said, "Lan' sakes, they sure ain't very big, are they?"

A tall, black-haired boy came into the room carrying two pails of milk. "This is my son, Bucky," Mrs. Stamens said.

Without looking at us, Bucky said, "Hey."

"Well, now I'll show you girls to your room and then get some supper ready," Mrs. Stamens said. The room upstairs was small and bare. "This double bed will do just fine," she said, "specially since you are such little things." Then she told us to hang up our coats and come down to the kitchen where it was warm.

After she left, we stood in silence. I walked to the window and looked out. How strange not to hear or see children. I watched some chickens peck at the frozen ground. Two horses stood silhouetted against the evening sky, occasionally swishing their tails. The cows waited motionless by the barn door. Plowed fields—scattered with the remnants of last year's harvest—stretched to the darkening sky. Far off I saw a light come on in a small grey house. Looking closely, I could see two figures inside.

They appeared to be children, and my hopes rose slightly. Dusk quickly followed the short twilight, and soon I could see in the windowpane only the reflection of my sisters standing beside me.

I looked at Carolyn's woebegone face and the pain in Betty's eyes, and asked, "Where are we?" Betty said she heard the woman in black call it a "foster home."

When I asked how long we would be here, Betty answered with a sigh, "Probably not very long." There was no certainty in her voice now, and her face was expressionless. She had not moved from the spot where she stood holding Carolyn's hand when the old woman left, and I knew she was as bewildered as I.

The room suddenly felt cold. We put our suitcases under the double bed, hung up our coats, and went down to the warm kitchen.

Mrs. Stamens had set plates on the table and was taking something from the oven of a big black stove. Mr. Stamens was sitting just where we had left him. Bucky sat down at the table and said, "Let's eat." There was cornbread, grits and milk that night, and almost every night thereafter.

"You young'uns go to school?" asked Bucky. Betty told him that she and I did. He proudly said that he drove the school bus. "That's it out in the yard. I take one load in the mornings and two in the afternoon, and you can ride with me on both loads if you want." We did not know what he meant, but he looked so pleased that we agreed.

Mr. Stamens ate without saying a word. When he had finished, he put some wood on the fire in the stove, and sat in the chair he had been sitting in when we arrived. Taking a small white bag from his shirt pocket, he tugged at the yellow string on the bag and took out a piece of something brown, which he put in his mouth and proceeded to chew with pleasure.

Mrs. Stamens told us she had some papers we were to take to school the next morning. She asked if they had given us enough clothes, how long our mother had been dead, and if we ever saw our father. She seemed nervous. Standing behind my chair to pour some more milk, she put her hand gently on my shoulder, and I felt a warmness go through me. I decided I could not call her Ma, but I knew I did not dislike her.

After the meal was finished, Mrs. Stamens told us to get our coats and she would show us the outhouse. Not knowing what she meant, we followed as she led the way with a flashlight. At a small structure a short distance from the house she said, "You girls go in one at a time and go to the bathroom." How odd to have a separate building for going to the bathroom, I thought. Waiting my turn, I was aware of the stillness, the unfamiliar smells, and the total darkness all around us. "Guess you girls ain't never seen an outhouse before," she said, breaking the silence. "Out here in the country we don't have no indoor plumbing," she added, in an effort to explain this to us.

Returning to the house, we were told where the flashlight was kept if we needed it during the night. I decided I would never go to that place alone in the darkness.

Then Mrs. Stamens filled a pan with water, and standing in the kitchen—with Bucky and Mr. Stamens looking on—we carefully washed our faces. Mrs. Stamens asked if we needed any help getting ready for bed. When we told her we didn't, she said goodnight, Mr. Stamens nodded, Bucky gave a wave, and we went upstairs.

When I opened my suitcase to get my nightgown, I saw Emily looking up at me with her big red smile. How glad I was to see her. I held her up and said, "How do you like this place, Emily?" Then I sat on the cold wooden floor and laughed out loud.

In the next room I could hear Mr. and Mrs. Stamens getting ready for bed. "Ma, guess you are going to have your hands full with them three young'uns," said Mr. Stamens.

"It's not going to be so bad. Seems to me they're pretty much able to look after themselves—guess you noticed how that older one never takes her eyes off the little one," I heard her reply.

"Think they are going to be worth the fifteen dollars a month we'll be getting?"

"Yep, I'm sure they will be."

The big bed was soft and quite warm as we snuggled together. Carolyn said she was hungry, but she was so exhausted that she quickly fell asleep. "I guess we are too far away now for Daddy to ever find us again," Betty whispered to me.

The last time I had seen my father—at the hospital—seemed so long ago and far away. Our big house, the sound of my mother's voice, the smell of the lilac bush, and the laughter of my father—memories of those times traveled through my mind and disappeared. In their place were the faces of Sister Catherine, the lady in lavender, Tom, and the woman in black. I fell asleep listening to nightbirds and telling myself that my father would surely find us here and take us home.

———————

At dawn we were awakened by a new sound which I learned was a rooster. We went to the outhouse together. After a breakfast of milk, biscuits, and jam, Betty and I boarded the big yellow bus and rode off, leaving Carolyn waving to us from the kitchen window.

Winding along dirt roads, the bus stopped here and there picking up children. They all seemed to know each other, and joked and laughed all the way to school. As we got off the bus a tall boy with a pimply face pointed to Betty and me and said to Bucky, "Hey, where'd you pick these up?"

"They live at my house," said Bucky.

"Relatives, eh?" asked the boy.

"No, they are orphans," answered Bucky.

"Well, now if that don't beat all," said the boy. "Why would your ma and pa take on a bunch of orphans when they ain't got enough money for themselves?"

Bucky clenched his fist and took a step forward. "Mind your own business."

Bucky told Betty and me that he would help us find our rooms. "And be sure to come straight to the bus when school is over," he added, so he wouldn't be late leaving with his first load.

Walking down the hallway of the school, I was grateful to Bucky for going with me, although I could tell he was embarrassed. The teacher was pleasant and the day went well. There were some stares and remarks like, "Where'd *you* come from?" but I decided to wait and see what happened later.

As I left school that first day, I went out a side door and spotted the most unusual swings. There was a tall pole with chains hanging down from it, and on each chain were two bars for holding on. Children were swinging round and round in maypole fashion. I had to try it. Putting my books down, I darted between two children, grabbed a bar and began to pump hard with my feet. I was soon flying high above the ground. The sensation of freedom was incredible as I sailed through the air, seeing objects on the ground flying past me at a dizzying speed.

I don't know how long Bucky had been calling me, but suddenly I saw him far below with his hands cupped to his mouth. Slowing the swing, I jumped off, picked up my books and ran toward him. He grabbed me by the arm, "You better listen to me, girl," he said, "when I tell you to go straight to that bus after school." My legs wobbled and my head was spinning from the motion of the swing, but I promised I would not make him late again.

Bucky pushed me onto the bus. "Having trouble with your orphans?" asked the pimply faced boy. Bucky's face reddened. Without a word, he shifted the bus into gear and we headed home.

Betty was furious with me and said I could have been left there all night. I tried to think about how awful that would be, but mostly I thought about how I could find a way to swing again.

As we neared the house, I could see Carolyn still sitting at the window. She was so small and alone, and it was on her that most of my fears centered. She never spoke up—never asked for anything, nor would she refuse something offered her she did not want. To be left alone in this strange place without Betty or me was a terrible experience, I was sure. Whenever Carolyn had cried since our mother died, I had wanted to run, to escape, to be away from all that was happening to us. Now seeing that small figure with her nose pressed against the window, waiting for us, I felt that my chest would explode.

Jumping off the bus and running to the house, I tried to think of a story to tell her. I wanted so much to hear her laugh as she used to. Then I saw she had not moved from her place by the window. In her arms was a little grey kitten.

"That old cat has kittens twenty times a year out there in the barn," said Mrs. Stamens. Then she looked at

Betty. "The child has not stirred from that chair all day. Hope you don't mind, I gave her the kitten to play with."

She had not been alone after all—she had a kitten, and it would keep her company while we were gone. "No ma'am," said Betty.

When we asked Carolyn what she was going to name the kitten, she said, "Just Kitty."

Bucky asked if we would like to go to the barn with him while he did his chores. The thought of going where those big animals were scared me a bit, but we followed him. Giving me a handful of corn, Bucky showed me how to call the chickens and scatter the corn. "Here chick, chick, chick," he called, and chickens came from every direction. "Better keep your eye on that old fella—he's a mean one," Bucky said pointing to a big yellow rooster.

We watched while Bucky forked hay into a wooden trough for the horses. He fed the two cows, and while they ate, he milked them. All the while, he explained to us what he was doing and why.

"Those old mules ain't good for nothin' but plowin'. And them chickens is the dumbest things the Lord ever made, but Ma says we need 'em to sell the eggs."

I could tell he had real affection for the cows, though. He had given them names, and he talked to them as if they were people. His hands were big and roughened by hard work, but they seemed so gentle as he milked.

My sisters and I went with Bucky most days and helped him with the chores. In an offhand way he told us how he disliked the farm and wanted to live in the city when he finished school. "I don't aim to be poor all my life," he said.

I learned to like the smell of the dried hay and the quiet times in the barn with Bucky while he milked. And I was beginning to lose my fear of the animals when one day, as

I was scattering corn for the chickens, the huge yellow rooster came strutting toward me. Spreading its wings downward until they almost reached the ground, it came closer. His head was held high and the bright red on top seemed to enlarge. I let out a scream and dropped the pail of corn just as the rooster threw itself at my leg and buried its spur deep in my ankle.

When Bucky carried me into the house with blood coming in spurts, Mrs. Stamens' face went white. She painted the cut with iodine and bandaged my ankle, but the pain persisted for days. I feared that rooster for as long as I lived with the Stamens', and still have the scar from his attack.

Mr. Stamens would come into the kitchen every evening before mealtime, take off his heavy boots and big coat, and pour himself some coffee. Without directing his conversation to anyone, he talked about his day. "Been chopping wood over at the Turner place," he sometimes announced.

He wore bibbed overalls, and when he crossed his legs you could see long underwear pulled down over dark socks. His face was unshaven, and his grey hair touseled. He had the look of someone who had seen many hard times and was now resigned to doing odd jobs for others, some farming in the summer, and sitting in the kitchen of his small house on cold nights. I never saw him read a newspaper, but he loved his radio. "Lum and Abner" was his favorite program, and he always listened to the evening news. Afterward, he commented on what President Roosevelt had done that day. "That John L. Lewis is a sonofagun for that strike," he would say. He loved the

President, and anyone the President disliked, he did not care for either.

Bucky liked "Gangbusters" and "The Major Bowes Amateur Hour." We all sat around the kitchen table listening to these programs, then the fire in the big stove would be banked, we would one by one go to the outhouse, and then upstairs to bed.

Huddling together under the quilts in the big bed, my sisters and I whispered until we fell asleep. Our conversations were always a guessing game. Would our daddy find us here? If not, where would we go next? Maybe Aunt Carrie would come for us. Why did the woman in black take us away from our daddy? The enigma of it all was unbearable.

One night before we went to sleep, Betty asked, "Do you know what tomorrow is, Anne?" When I said I did not, she said, "It's your seventh birthday."

Betty's birthday in July had gone unnoticed at the orphanage, but when she had told us that summer day that she was now eight years old, I had looked at her and thought "How old and smart she is." Carolyn and I had sung "Happy Birthday" to her, and I knew they would do the same for me tomorrow.

There was little to separate one day from the next as winter went on. I began to dislike school more than ever. The children were cruel. Except for making faces at them, I had not done much to defend myself. Their attacks were usually verbal and not physical. But anger burned in me until one day in March, when one of the girls called me a "dirty little orphan" I pulled her down to the ground and hit her with all my strength. She screamed, and before I could move, her brother came at me and struck me square in the jaw. Reeling backward, I landed so hard on the ground that my new glasses fell off. I got up and went after him wildly. "I'm not a dirty orphan," I screamed as I tore at his face, arms, and shirt. I could see blood coming from his cheek, and I suddenly felt sick. "Leave me alone," I cried as I picked up my glasses and ran into the school.

My teacher, Miss Percy, made me sit in the hall for the rest of the afternoon. The first day I was in her class, I had thought she was the most beautiful lady I had ever seen. She wore soft knitted sweaters and pleated skirts, and when she walked the pleats swayed back and forth. Her long blonde hair was sometimes done up in thick braids across the top of her head, at other times it was held back with silver combs.

But I had noticed from the beginning that she never called on me to recite, and if I raised my hand she ignored me. One rainy cold morning the children were standing by the radiator to dry off before class began. When one of the girls complained that there was no room for her, Miss Percy had said, "Anne, why don't you give her your place?"

Now sitting in the hall with my dress torn, my glasses so crooked I could not see properly, and my jaw aching, I decided I hated them all.

When I got on the bus after school, I tried to sneak past Bucky, but he caught me by the arm and said, "What happened to you?"

Jerking away from him I said, "Nothing." I sat close to Betty all the way home. How good it felt to be near her and feel the silent love between us.

Mrs. Stamens was horrified when she saw me. "Lord sakes, what happened?" she asked, her voice louder than I had ever heard it. Then she made me sit in front of her and tell the story while Bucky stood there and listened.

"You better never fight again," said Mrs. Stamens as she gave me a cloth to wash my face. "I'm responsible for you and if you ever get hurt bad, that lady who brung you out here will have the law on me. Girls ain't supposed to fight anyway."

Mrs. Stamens was not one to get upset. Her pace in life was slow, she did what she had to do each day—never complaining and never rejoicing. When she asked a question like, "How did your day go?" in her low monotonous voice, it was out of politeness, not interest. I was aware that she paid no attention to the answers.

That day as she washed my bruised face, I could sense that somewhere in her frail body there would be a torrent of anger if unleashed. Pushing back her hair and holding her palm across her forehead as if to quell a headache, she said in sharp, halting words, "Go change that dress and bring it down so's I can mend it."

Going upstairs, I could see the long oval mirror in the corner of Mrs. Stamens' room. Other than passing through the parlor, as it was called, we had never since our arrival been in any room except the kitchen and our bedroom. Making sure I was alone, I tiptoed up to the big mirror and looked at myself for the first time in a long while.

I could see they were right. I was nothing but a dirty orphan. My hair had not been shampooed since I left the orphanage, and it hung in limp strands down the sides of my face. My jaw was turning purple, my glasses were so askew I had to hold them up on my nose to see, the sleeves of my underwear hung below the sleeves of my dress, a new front tooth was coming in crooked, and my socks fell around those awful brown shoes, revealing my bony legs and ankles. "Oh, Mother," I thought, "if you could see me now."

Dressing her three little girls had been one of the pleasures of her life. Our dresses were always starched, our shoes polished, and our hair done in Shirley Temple style. After brushing each little curl carefully into place, Mother would stand us in front of Daddy and say, "Aren't they beautiful?"

I pulled my hair back, tucked my underwear sleeves under the dress, tugged up my socks, and was trying to get a better view of myself through my tilted glasses when Mrs. Stamens called, "Hurry up with that dress." I went quickly into my room.

Before changing, I took Emily out of the suitcase and propped her up on the pillows. "Well, Emily I've done it again, and I don't feel one bit better for it." She looked so pretty sitting there with her big smile, her clean dress, and the green Christmas ribbon still in her hair. "I'm not going to let you get like me."

Giving the dress to Mrs. Stamens, I put on my coat and went out to the barn with Bucky. "With that jaw and those broken glasses you do look funny, girl," he said. He took his little stool, sat down and started to milk. I sat on the ground beside him. Cupping my sore jaw in my cold hand, I asked him, "Why don't they like me, Bucky?"

" 'Cause you are different," he said.

"Why am I different?"

"You're an orphan, girl."

"Are Betty and I the only orphans at the school?"

"Probably."

"Why are we orphans when we don't live at the orphanage anymore?"

" 'Cause you ain't got no mother and daddy, and you got to live with other folks."

Getting up I shouted, "I do have a daddy!"

"Now calm down, girl," said Bucky. "O.K., you got a daddy, but right now he ain't taking care of you." Then he got up and came over to where I was, sat down on a truss of straw and said softly, "Why don't you stop fighting—it don't matter what people call you."

"It does matter, Bucky. Why don't you hit that pimply-faced boy on the bus who kept making you mad?"

"You mean old Doug Turner? Why, he ain't worth my time. He thinks just cause his folks got a bit more money and land than mine he's better than me. What he's really mad about is I got to drive the bus and he didn't." Bucky said this as if he thought it was funny.

Returning to his milking, he added, "Instead of wastin' your time fightin', why don't you make them like you?"

While he finished, I nursed my sore face and thought about what he had said. There were some boys who played marbles at recess, and Tom had admitted I was as good as he was—if I just had some marbles.

"Bucky, you got any marbles?"

"I might," he said, looking confused.

Later that evening, when I had washed my hair in a pan on the kitchen table—determined to look my best the next day—Bucky gave me six marbles.

"What do you know about marbles?" he asked.

"A lot."

"Let's see what you can do." He kneeled on the kitchen floor.

Using one of the migs because I liked the size and feel of it, I got down on the floor and gave it my best shot.

"Not too bad, but get down lower so you really eyeball it," he said.

After half an hour of practice, Bucky said, "Doggone, girl I believe you can beat 'em."

Mrs. Stamens looked up from her mending, "Don't go puttin' notions in that girl's head."

A few days before, I had watched Mr. Stamens empty one of his little white bags with the yellow string on it—and asked if I could have it. It smelled strong, but I put it in my suitcase. Now I decided it was the perfect sack for my marbles.

The next day, with clean hair and the marbles rattling in my coat pocket, I could hardly wait for recess. Getting into the game wasn't easy.

"Hey, look, the orphan wants to play," someone chanted.

"I've got some marbles and I can play as well as you," I said.

"Let her try," one of the boys snickered.

Six boys each placed a marble in the circle, and laughed as I knelt down. Getting at eye level, I put my blue marble in the crook of my thumb and forefinger, and shot into the circle. To their surprise—and somewhat to my own—I shot out four of their marbles. After that it was fair play, and I went home with seventeen new marbles. By the end of the week I had thirty-two marbles in the little white bag in my suitcase. The boys accepted me now, although they still called me "the orphan."

My triumph ended when a new boy appeared at the game. He was tall and scruffy, wearing a ragged, red-plaid mackinaw, and he kicked me from behind as I knelt to shoot. "Bet you can't beat me," he challenged.

The rest of the boys sat back as the tall boy placed four marbles in the circle. First shot I took two of his. And by the time recess ended he had only four marbles left. He wasn't happy, and as I reached for my last win, his foot came down hard on my hand. "You ain't gonna' keep those."

Yanking my hand away, I pulled both of his legs and he fell backward. He was head and shoulders taller than me, and while he twisted my arm and pulled my hair, I kicked him hard.

A circle of children stood around cheering us on, until

Miss Percy separated us. Pulling me by the arm into the classroom, she said, "How did you get yourself into *this* fight?" Without waiting for my answer, she made me hold out my hand and gave me ten hard licks with her ruler.

Later in the barn, I told Bucky about the fight. "How come you let him pin your arms behind you?" he wanted to know.

"I couldn't help it!"

"Looks like you got some learnin' to do," he said, kneeling down in front of me.

"What are you going to do?"

"Teach you how to fight, girl—if you ain't gonna stay outa trouble, you might as well know how to take care of yourself."

His face was at eye level, and looking into his brown eyes I felt my anger and hatred slipping away. Nothing about Bucky was like my father, but with him I had a comfortable feeling I had shared only with my father.

"Now hit me," he said.

I made a clumsy effort to strike him, but without anger I could not do it.

"First thing you gotta learn, girl, is lead with your right."

Making a fist with my right hand, I tried to hit him, but he had already punched me.

Then he showed me how to watch both his hands. If his left arm was up, punch him in the stomach with my right. Then we worked on the left hand using the same procedure, and we practiced until Mrs. Stamens called us for supper. Walking toward the house carrying pails of milk, Bucky said, "Don't ever bite and scratch—that's girl stuff. Just lead with your right and watch the other fella's hands all the time."

Bucky's technique worked, and for the remainder of

first grade I feared no one except Miss Percy, who punished me often. I would not want to think about my grades that year or how I managed to be promoted.

———————

Summer came, and I found there was more to this place than the little white house and the barn. There were acres and acres of plowed fields. Mr. Stamens talked about corn and cotton, and Mrs. Stamens sat on the back screened porch while she shelled beans. Bucky came in from the fields for lunch with his shoes dusty and sweat pouring from his body. Betty had a friend up the road, and she went there often to play. Carolyn and I took turns swinging in the old tire Bucky had hung from a tree for us.

On a hot day we took turns pumping water while the other one stood under the pump, squealing with delight as the first gush splashed on her head. A few times Bucky let us ride in the back of the pickup truck when he took his mother to the store. It was a long, bumpy, and adventurous ride. While Mrs. Stamens made her purchases, Bucky bought each of us a grape drink and told us to wait on the store steps.

Summer was lazy and monotonous until one day I took a walk down a narrow path through the hay field. At the end of the path was the little grey house I had seen from the window that first night. Beside the house was a black woman, singing and stirring something in a big pot. Two black children, a boy and a girl, were dancing in rhythm to her song. When they saw me, they stopped and hid behind her.

"Hello there," said the lady, "Where'd you come from?"

"I live back there." I pointed.

"You must be one of the little ones who lives with the

Stamens I heard about," she said, "Well, it's nice of you to come over here, but you best git on back home."

"Could your children play with me?" I asked.

"Mrs. Stamens ain't gonna like you goin' off and playin' with us folks." Then holding each of her children by the hand, she came over to me and said, "Long as you're here, might as well have a glass of something to drink—such a hot day."

Her name was Emma Watson, she told me, and her children were Thadeus, called Thad, and Sara Jane.

"Sit here on the porch, children, while I get some tea," Emma said.

Thad would not look at me and kept fiddling with a branch on the tree, listening for his mother to return. But Sara Jane gave me a big grin and asked if I'd like to see their new calf. "She was jus' born last night. Mama says we gotta' watch her close all day 'cause she come early."

Sara Jane had a body so nimble I envied her. In a race she always won, and I felt clumsy alongside her as we climbed trees. She had a dance for every song. Her good nature was infectious, and we quickly became friends. Thad was thoughtful. He wanted to be a baseball player and spent his time tossing a ball in the air and hitting it with his bat. Sometimes Sara Jane and I played roll-a-bat with him. Thad was always first to bat. After he hit the ball, Sara Jane and I would scramble to catch it—the one catching it got to roll the ball to where Thad had laid the bat on the ground. If the ball hit the bat, then that person was batter.

Emma could fill the world with her songs and her love. All she had were two children, a hardworking husband and a shanty, but her smooth brown face showed no signs of stress or unhappiness. She often joined in games with Thad, Sara Jane, and me, and sometimes she sat in her rocking chair on the porch and told us stories. Every afternoon when I was there she made a milk shake for us with milk, sugar, and vanilla. I thought it was delicious. And I remember the hot summer day she sat under the grape arbor with Sara Jane and me and showed us how to make a daisy chain.

One day Emma took me on her lap and asked me about my mother and father. Laying my head against her clean apron and feeling her strong arms around me, I told her everything. When I told her about Doug Turner starting the orphan story at school, she threw back her head and laughed. "Land sakes, he got holes in his socks jus' like the rest of us—I know 'cause I does their family laundry." Then she hummed softly as she rocked me and said, "Don't you worry none—the Lord's gonna take care of you and your sisters. Everybody has to suffer sometimes. Guess you is gittin' yours now."

I did not tell Mrs. Stamens about my visits to Emma's house. One afternoon there was a thunderstorm, and it was getting dark when the rain slacked off enough for me to return to the Stamens. "She gonna be awful worried about you, but when she ask where you been, be truthful," Emma said. But no questions were asked when I walked in the Stamens' kitchen and took my place at the table for supper.

———

One evening just before bedtime Bucky said, "Sure wish we had somebody to help us get that cotton in."

"Tom Watson is gonna help tomorrow," his father replied.

My sisters and I had never seen cotton growing, so we asked Bucky if we could go with him the next morning. "O.K.," he said, "but if you ride over to the field with me in the truck, you gotta stay til I'm ready to come home."

That was fine with us—it meant a ride in the truck and getting away from the house for a day.

Next morning Bucky loaded the back of his pickup with piles of burlap, and with the three of us up front with him, drove to the cotton fields about a mile away. They were beautiful—rows of snowy fluffy balls of cotton stretching to the horizon. "Could we help you pick?" I asked.

"Maybe," he said, as he got the burlap out of the truck and laid pieces of it flat at the end of each row of cotton. Next he began to pick the cotton, showing us how to get the whole ball loose from the hard petals surrounding it, and dropped it into a big cloth sack. "If you pick it out bit by bit, it ain't no good."

It was easy, and my sisters and I held up our skirts, making a basket to carry the cotton we picked. When our skirts were full, we ran to the end of the row and emptied the cotton into the burlap.

Mr. Stamens came along and I heard him say to Bucky, "Hey, them girls is doin' all right—they don't even have to bend over. Maybe they ain't so useless after all."

After that we spent most of our days in the cotton fields as the late August sun boiled down on us—turning our bodies bronze—and the hot red dirt scorched the soles of our feet.

I began to feel tired all the time. At first I tried to ignore it, and went to bed early, hoping to feel better the next day. Carolyn ate less, and Betty's and my appetites also diminished. Finally one evening, I got out of the truck—after picking cotton all day—and fainted. When I came to, Mrs. Stamens and Bucky were standing over me, and Betty and Carolyn were sitting beside me, ashen-faced. "She's just tuckered out from the hot sun," Mrs. Stamens said. "She'll be all right by mornin'"

But I wasn't all right, and Betty and Carolyn felt as

listless as I. We did not go back to the cotton fields anymore, and a few days later the woman in black showed up. She looked at us with more than usual interest and asked Mrs. Stamens, "What is the problem?"

"They don't have no appetite and they are tired all the time," replied Mrs. Stamens. "Maybe I ain't doin' right by keepin' them here."

"Oh, they'll be all right—we'll let the doctor have a look at them and I'll bring them back soon," the woman in black assured her.

The ride into Charlotte to the public health clinic was long and tiring, but when we reached the city I sat forward in my seat and looked out the window. We passed the theater where we had once spent our Saturday mornings, the big department stores with people hurrying in and out, the dime store where our father had let us buy chocolate balls. At the end of the main street I saw the Wimpy hamburger sign, and wondered if my father still had his supper there. Somewhere in this strange but familiar place was my father, and my eyes searched the streets for him.

When the doctor completed his examination, he said to the woman in black, "These girls are suffering from anemia."

"What does that mean?" she asked.

"It means they need some good red meat and lots of rest, which I doubt they are getting."

"Now what am I going to do with them?"

"You might try a lady who is a nurse. She sometimes takes cases like this," he said, writing a name on a piece of paper and handing it to her.

As we were leaving, Betty asked the woman in black, "Do you think we could visit our daddy while we are here?"

"Heavens no, child, that is out of the question," she said and hurried us back toward the car.

Back at the farm, she and Mrs. Stamens talked for a long time in the parlor while we sat in the kitchen and told Bucky about our trip to the city.

About a month after this, Mrs. Stamens said as we sat at supper, "Well, girls, looks like you will be leaving us."

"Where are we going?" asked Betty.

"They are going to put you in a home with a nurse who will make you healthy again," she said, looking a bit sad.

The next morning I ran all the way to Emma's house.

"Well, hello there, Anne. What brings you down here so early?" Emma asked.

"We're leaving tomorrow."

"Is your daddy comin' for you?" she asked with a big smile.

"No," I said, not looking at her.

Her smile disappeared for a moment. Then she clapped her hands. "Sara Jane, git out the white tablecloth—we is gonna' have a goin'-away party for Anne."

She made large glasses of the milk shake, opened a jar of her own blackberries, and put out a plate of cookies. Then she told me to sit on the porch for a minute while they got the rest of the party ready. When I returned, there were three gifts at my place, each wrapped in white paper and tied with various colors of yarn. In the center of the table was a single candle in a clay holder that I had watched her make. It all looked so festive that I felt like a queen.

My gift from Sara Jane was a necklace made of pecan shells, Thad gave me two pennies in a tiny match box, and Emma gave me a handkerchief with a small rosebud embroidered in the corner. When I told Emma I wished I had something for them, she said that would not be right.

71

"It ain't often we has a friend who comes to visit every day and then has to go away."

Before I left, Emma sat me on her lap and told me not to be afraid. "The Lord ain't gonna' give his children more than they can bear."

As she held me close, she started to sing. "Do you know 'Annie Laurie'?" I asked. "This was my father's song for me."

> "Maxwelton's braes are bonnie,
> Where airley falls the dew.
> And 'twas there that Annie Laurie
> Gave me her promise true."

Emma sang in her deep contralto voice.

"I wish they would let me stay with you," I said.

"Well, they ain't never gonna' do that—but I really loves you, chile," she said as she held me closer.

"I love you too, Emma."

When I left she told me not to look back, but not to forget her too soon.

As I neared the barn, I did turn to look once more at the little grey house, and dried my tears on my new handkerchief before I went up to my room to pack my suitcase.

The next morning we sat on the front porch with our suitcases, waiting for the woman in black. Mr. Stamens sat in his rocking chair, half-dozing. Bucky leaned against the porch rail, saying nothing. Mrs. Stamens sat on the steps, and occasionally patted one of us or brushed back our hair with her hand. "You are fine little girls," she said, "and you are going to grow up strong." After a long pause, added, "Hope it ain't been too bad livin' out here with us."

Carolyn was holding "Kitty," who was now a big grey cat. My strength had come from Betty's endurance, but I knew from the way she was pacing around with her thoughtful look that she was as uneasy as I about what was to come next.

The woman in black arrived, and Bucky put the suitcases in the car. Mrs. Stamens gave us a disconcerted hug, saying, "Y'all be good girls."

Mr. Stamens called out goodbye from his place on the porch. Bucky dug his hands into his overall pockets and said, "I'm gonna' miss you young'uns." Just before I got in the car, he reached out and pulled a strand of my hair. "Remember, girl, always lead with your right."

Mrs. Stamens gave him a puzzled look, then walked into the house.

As we rode away I looked back. Mr. and Mrs. Stamens had disappeared, but the figure of the tall farm boy, standing on the dirt road waving goodbye to us, will be in my memory forever.

CHAPTER V

~~~~~~~~~~~~~~~~~~~~~~~~~~~~~~~~

The neat white house surrounded by tall pines was an hour's drive further into the country. A blue October sky, a gentle breeze lightly twisting the yellow leaves of a giant oak, made it all look so peaceful, and yet terrifying.

Walking up the steps to a porch that went halfway around the house, I felt a chill. I had heard the doctor at the clinic say this woman was a nurse, and I visualized her in white, with tongue depressors, thermometer, and needle. But I had not expected her to live in a house like this—so isolated from the rest of the world.

The woman in black knocked several times. Then the door was opened by a tall, heavyset woman with tight black curls and a wide mouth. She was not wearing a white uniform, but a red print dress with long sleeves. Her white shoes were laced close around her thick ankles.

When she spoke, my sisters and I moved closer together. "Hello," she said in a loud, raspy voice. "Come on inside, I don't want the flies to come in. Soon as the weather gets cooler, I have a time with these flies."

We stepped into a room that was large, well-furnished, and smelled faintly of disinfectant. There was a piano with a framed picture of a pretty girl on top of it, a blue velvet sofa with antimacassars that looked new. The polished tables and lamps with gold-fringed shades reminded me of pictures from a Sears catalogue I had found in the trash at the orphanage.

"Well, now let's get acquainted," said the loud woman.

"This is Betty, Anne, and Carolyn," said the woman in black. To us she said, "This is Mrs. Coburn."

Walking slowly around us with her hands on her hips, Mrs. Coburn said, "My, they are pathetic looking, aren't they?" Then she added, "But don't you worry, I'll fatten them up in no time."

She had just about made full circle around us when a boy came into the room, "Mama, Mama, I was looking for you!"

He seemed frantic, and his speech was thick and slurred. He was almost as tall as his mother, with sandy hair, a round pink face, and bulging blue eyes.

"This is my son, Benny," said Mrs. Coburn. She told him who we were, and that we were going to stay with them for awhile.

"Girls! I like girls!" he exclaimed, jumping up and down. As he came toward us, we looked at each other and backed away. Seeing the three suitcases, he sat on the floor and tried to undo them. I grabbed mine and held it behind me. "I want it, I want it!" he screamed.

"Now girls, we must learn to share with Benny," his mother said.

"I really must be going," said the woman in black.

Benny suddenly lost interest in the suitcases and went over to her. He put his arm around her and said, "You're nice."

Moving away from him and heading for the door, she told Mrs. Coburn, "Call me if you need me," and left.

Mrs. Coburn hurried us out of the immaculate parlor, closed and locked the door, and led us to our room. Benny followed and again became interested in the suitcases. When he tried to take mine, I yanked it away and said, "Leave it alone!" His mother gave me an icy stare, but said nothing to Benny.

The room that was to be ours contained three narrow iron beds, a straight-backed chair, and nothing more. The stark white walls, scrubbed barren floor, and the smell of disinfectant that pervaded the house brought back memories of the hospital. I shuddered.

"Do you have your clothes in those suitcases?" asked Mrs. Coburn.

When Betty said that we did, she told us to open them up. I had never shared the contents of my suitcase with anyone and to do it now with this stranger was impossible. Turning my back, I quickly took out my clothes, shut the suitcase and put it under the bed.

Mrs. Coburn was watching me closely and said, "Let me see that doll you have there."

Carefully opening the suitcase just enough to get Emily out, I held her up for Mrs. Coburn to see.

"Do all of you have dolls like this?" she asked, snatching Emily from me.

Betty and Carolyn replied that we did. Mrs. Coburn took the three dolls and examined them. "I'll have to put them out in the sun tomorrow to kill any germs they may be carrying," she said with disgust.

Then she went through our clothes, picking them up gingerly with her fingers. "These will have to be boiled," she said as she put them in a pile.

"The first thing I want you girls to do is wash your faces and hands, then you can sit quietly in the kitchen while I start supper."

Showing us to the bathroom, she told us we must clean the basin after we had washed. Then she left to check on Benny.

"I hate her," I told Betty.

"We'll have to wait and see," Betty said.

"I'm scared of Benny," Carolyn said.

Mrs. Coburn soon returned and led us to the kitchen, which was as clean as the rest of the house. There were no dusty shoes by the door and no coats hung over chairs, as there had been at the Stamens' house. The table was set for six and the food smelled good, though my stomach was churning.

Benny was sitting on a high stool, but when he saw us he jumped off and came over. Using the little finger of his left hand, he tapped Betty on the forehead and asked, "Is the moon gonna' shine all night, chap?" For reasons never explained, he called us "chaps" for as long as we lived there.

Betty moved away from him, and her manner for the moment lost the dignity that had always marked her movements. Her revulsion did not dampen his enthusiasm, and he repeated the question louder. My sisters and I looked at each other and said nothing. Benny started to cry, and his mother asked Betty angrily, "Why don't you answer him?"

"Because I don't know the answer," Betty said, gritting her teeth and trying to be polite.

"Then why don't you just say yes and make him happy?" said Mrs. Coburn.

Again Benny asked, "Is the moon gonna' shine all night, chap?" and this time Betty said yes.

"Oh, goody," said Benny. "Then the ghosts will be out."

As Benny danced around the kitchen, an outside door

opened and a man came in. He was of medium height, with brown hair and a kindly face.

Benny ran to him and said, "Daddy, Daddy, see the chaps!"

Mrs. Coburn said, "Girls, this is my husband, Mr. Coburn." She told him our names and remarked about how unhealthy-looking we were.

Mr. Coburn said, "Hello, girls, I'm glad to meet you." His voice was soft and his manner timid. Like a well-trained child he hung up his coat, washed his hands, and sat down for supper.

My sisters and I sat on one side of the table facing Benny, with Mr. and Mrs. Coburn sitting at either end. We bowed our heads while Mrs. Coburn said a lengthy blessing—a few words of thanks for the food, and then a long plea asking for help in restoring health to these poor homeless children.

During the meal Mrs. Coburn reminded us over and over how nourishing the food was, and that we had to eat every bite on our plates before we could leave the table. Mr. Coburn, his napkin tucked in his collar, ate quietly.

Benny devoured his food. "I want more! I want more!" he bellowed.

Throughout the meal he stared at my sisters and me. His face was a mixture of cupidity and hostility. I wanted to escape from his gaze, to shut out the sound of his voice. But I knew that as long as we stayed here, he would be here too, and I had to find a way to survive it.

After dinner, Mr. Coburn lit his pipe, said "Goodnight, son" to Benny, nodded to us and Mrs. Coburn, and went to his room. Mrs. Coburn called out, "Don't forget to polish your shoes." Turning to us, she said, "All right, girls, get this kitchen cleaned up."

When we looked at each other wondering what she

meant, she shouted, "Well don't just stand there—Betty, you can wash the dishes; Anne, you dry; and Carolyn can sweep.

All the while we worked Benny sat on the high stool and stared at us like an animal about to pounce. Occasionally he patted the top of his head, swung his legs fiercely, or waved his arms, but he stayed on the stool until our cleaning was finished.

Then Mrs. Coburn told us to take a bath and get into bed. "Be quick about it, because I have to give you your medicine and we have to have our reading."

As we prepared for bed, Betty said, "It's nice she is going to read to us."

"I still don't like her," I said.

Mrs. Coburn came into the room carrying a large bottle of dark brown medicine, a tablespoon, and a Bible.

"All right, girls, line up in front of me and take your medicine," she said, her wide mouth curved into a smile. The thick syrupy bitterness made me gag, but I turned away from her and held my hand over my mouth until the feeling went away.

"Now girls, I want you to stand by your beds while I set down the rules for you." Marching back and forth across the room she began, "While you are here you must keep your room spotless. You will clean the kitchen after each meal. You will help with the laundry and any other chores I give you. You are not to annoy Benny—this is his home, not yours. You will not be going to school this winter because of your poor health, which means you will be in my care at all times, and I expect perfect behavior."

She hesitated and then said, "I have decided you will call me *Ma Mere*—that is French for Mother. Since you poor things do not have a mother, I thought you might like that."

Taking the straight-backed chair, she placed it between the beds, sat down and opened her Bible. "Get into bed now, and we will have our reading."

The bed felt good to my tired body, and I wished she would leave the room. But she went on. "We are going to read from the Book of Revelations—that is my favorite," she said with enthusiasm.

On that October evening, at the age of seven and a half, my introduction to the Bible began with this:

"And I stood upon the sand of the sea, and saw a beast rise up out of the sea, having seven heads and ten horns, and upon his horns ten crowns, and upon his heads the name of blasphemy. And the beast which I saw was like a leopard and his feet were as the feet of a bear, and his mouth as the mouth of a lion: and the dragon gave him his power, and his seat, and great authority."

The reading went on, but I put my hands under the pillow and brought it up over my ears so that I could hear no more.

Finally closing the Bible, Mrs. Coburn said, "Now out of your beds and kneel down while we pray."

She clasped her hands together, closed her eyes, and with her face turned upward, began, "Oh, Lord how we do love Thee—cleanse our souls—help us through this night. . ."

I watched her face as she prayed and felt that I was looking at a person different from the big garrulous woman I already despised. Had she opened her eyes then, she would not have been aware of her surroundings—her voice quivered and her body rocked back and forth as she continued her fervent implorations. The transformation was frightening, and I watched with amazement.

As she said "Amen," her body went limp and her head relaxed forward. Then she stood up, straightened her dress, and the jarring voice returned. "Into bed now, girls, and I don't want to hear a sound out of you until morning."

We lay in the darkened room unable to speak. I could hear Mrs. Coburn moving about, and for a short while there was silence. Then footsteps, and the sound of our door being opened. I saw a great white form come toward us and heard "Whoooo—whoooo" coming from it. The three of us watched, and as the form reached the foot of the beds we screamed. The form disappeared quickly from the room, and Mrs. Coburn appeared with curlers in her hair and wearing a robe.

"Now what is the meaning of this?" she asked angrily.

"There was a ghost in here," Betty said.

"How foolish to think that I'd believe something like that," she said.

"I saw it, too," said Carolyn.

"Shut up and go to sleep," said Mrs. Coburn as she walked out of the room and slammed the door behind her.

"What are we going to do?" I whispered to Betty.

"I don't know," Betty said. "Maybe we won't have to stay here too long," she added.

"Why don't they take us back to Daddy?" I asked.

"They will sometime," Betty answered.

"Will the ghost come again?" Carolyn wanted to know.

"I don't think so," Betty said, but I knew she was as scared as we were.

"Are you going to call her *Ma Mere*?" I asked.

"No," said Betty.

"Me neither," Carolyn said.

Moonlight filled the room, forming bizarre patterns on

the white wall and the ominous sound of a tree branch blowing against the house made me pull the covers up over my head. I wanted to remember happier days, but my confusion of thoughts would not let me. I pondered over the passage from the Bible about the beast with seven heads and ten horns, Benny's strange behavior, and Mrs. Coburn's praying. Then I thought of Emily tossed on the heap of clothes, and my emotional controls broke down. Burying my face in my pillow, I cried until I fell asleep.

There was only a rim of light along the morning horizon when Mrs. Coburen called to us to get up.

"There's much to be done today," she said as she hurried about the room, opening windows and yanking the covers off the beds.

I had dreamed all night of beasts with heads and horns. In my dream the beasts charged at me, and I was too weak to move. When they came nearer, I saw tight black curls on their heads and wide mouths stretching to devour me. I called out for help but no one answered.

Getting out of bed I trembled, remembering the dream. As I dressed I wondered, what would this day be like? What was there to be done from before the sun came up until it went down? Why could we not go to school? This was to be Carolyn's first year in school, and she had looked forward to it. Now she would miss first grade. She looked so small as she stood there dressing herself. I tried to remember her on my father's shoulders, her brown eyes shining as he made up ridiculous limericks for her. Her quiet good nature had changed to melancholy, her face was pale and her attitude wary.

Betty had finished dressing, and was brushing Carolyn's

hair. I watched her long slender fingers patiently untangle the curls, the flawless features of her face composed in deep thought. There was something majestic about her indomitable silence. I knew I had embarrassed her many times with my temper, but she never talked about it.

"How long ago did Mother die?" I asked as I tied my shoes.

"A year and a half," replied Betty. She kept a little calendar that Mrs. Stamens had given her. The numbers and days no longer matched, but she carefully checked off each day so that she could tell the date.

Just then Mrs. Coburn stuck her head in the door. "You are the slowest children I've ever seen—get in the kitchen and eat before your breakfast gets cold."

Benny was already at the table, gulping down his food. Mrs. Coburn told us she had to milk the cow, and for us to be nice to Benny while she was out. His repelling face broke into a clownish grin as he waved his arms at us. "I told you the ghost would come last night," he said.

Betty continued to eat, ignoring him. Carolyn's eyes widened with fright as she remembered the night before. I leaned forward, stuck out my tongue, crossed my eyes, and put my fingers in my ears. He crumpled in his chair and looked genuinely hurt when his mother returned.

"What's the matter, Benny?" she asked.

"She made a bad face at me," he said, pointing to me.

Setting down her pail of milk, she bent close to my face and said, "Now young lady, I thought I made it clear that you are not to bother Benny."

I studied the scowl on her face as she continued. "If you bother him one more time, you will spend the entire day in the springhouse alone."

In a quiet voice Betty said, "Benny was talking about the ghost again."

Turning to Betty, she became even more hostile. "I am speaking to your sister. I suppose the three of you will try to band together against me—well, I won't allow it."

In spite of her lecture, I knew she was a bit shaken, and when she lined us up for our medicine her hand trembled as she poured the brown liquid into the spoon.

The morning went quickly. We soon learned this was to be the pattern of all our days here. My sisters and I cleaned the kitchen as we had done the night before. Then we scrubbed the floor with pails of disinfectant. It took two of us to lift the pails, and if we halted for a moment in our work, Mrs. Coburn would say, "Come, come, girls, let's not waste time." Three final moppings were needed to please her.

"All right, outside now, girls," she ordered, and we marched off like soldiers on their first day at camp. Steam was rising from boiling water in a big black pot in the backyard. Beside the pot were three galvanized washtubs, each filled with water. There was a washboard standing in each tub, and Mrs. Coburn showed us how to use them. Betty was put at the last washtub, because Mrs. Coburn thought she could do a better job of the final wringing of the clothes. Then Mrs. Coburn took an old broom handle and began lifting the hot clothes out of the boiling water. I rinsed and scrubbed the clothes in my tub, then passed them to Carolyn, who also rinsed and scrubbed, then passed them on to Betty.

It was some weeks in coming, but we knew we had mastered the job when we were able to use those washboards without having our knuckles bleed.

When we had hung the clothes out to dry, we stopped for lunch. Benny had not taken part in the morning chores, but had lurked nearby for a while, disappearing once for a short time—his manner strange and distant. At times he talked to himself, then laughed hysterically or fell suddenly to the ground and seemed to look far off without seeing. Mrs. Coburn would give him a helpless look and go on about her work.

After lunch, we asked Mrs. Coburn if we could play with our dolls. "I guess so," she said. "They are out on the side porch."

We looked for them but could not find them. Reporting this to Mrs. Coburn, she said, "Well, that is where I put them. I haven't time to go searching for dolls. Go on outside and don't wander beyond the barn."

We had liked the old barn at the Stamens' place and decided to have a look at this one. A few feet from the barn we saw our dolls lying on the ground. We ran to pick them up and I looked with horror at Emily, lying half buried in the black damp earth. Her dress was gone, and only a few strands of the yarn were left on her head. Her pink face turned smudgy grey as I brushed away the dirt. Tears filled my eyes and I burned with rage.

Betty stared in disbelief at her doll, and Carolyn hugged hers as if to console it in this humiliating state.

"We must tell Mrs. Coburn about this," Betty said.

"Who did it?" I asked.

"It had to be Benny," she replied.

Mrs. Coburn gasped when she saw the dolls, but when Betty asked if Benny had done it, she jerked her shoulders back. "Let's not be making accusations." Looking at the dolls with a frown, she said. "Get those dirty things out of my kitchen."

I took Emily, wrapped her in a clean petticoat, and put her in my suitcase. On my way outside I paused by the kitchen door and heard Mrs. Coburn talking to Benny. She had her hands on his shoulders and was saying, "I want to know what you were doing with those dolls."

Benny said, "You know, Mama," and threw back his head, laughing.

Releasing her hold, she looked at him for a long time. Then in a low voice she said, "I should never have taken those three girls."

Throughout the evening meal Mrs. Coburn was silent. Rigid in her chair, she radiated both disagreeableness and tragedy. When the meal was finished, she said, "Get busy, girls, and be quick about it."

Mr. Coburn gave us a sympathetic look, said goodnight, and went to his room.

Benny sat on his stool watching us in a strange, stealthy way. Then bounding off the stool, he went to Betty and tapped her on the head, just as he had done the night before. "Moon gonna' shine all night, chap?"

"No," said Betty as she carried the dishes off the table.

Benny collapsed to the floor in loud, bellowing sobs. In an instant Mrs. Coburn appeared, and Benny told her what Betty had said. She knelt beside him, cradled his head in her lap, and told him the moon would shine all night. Then she told Betty she was never to disagree with Benny again. Betty said nothing.

Every night for the rest of our time at the Coburns, Benny would question one of us about the moon. Our answer was always yes, the moon would shine all night. The ghost would appear, and for the first week we cowered in fear of that great white form. Then one night we saw Benny standing in the corner of his room, placing a sheet over himself. We did not tell him that we knew his secret, and simply covered our heads with our blankets when he came in.

Each day after our morning chores were finished we went in search of a place to be away from Mrs. Coburn and Benny. The loft in the barn was a favorite spot. Betty brought her books and read to us—sometimes pretending she was a teacher and we were her students. At times we talked of our desperation to leave this strange place and of our hope of seeing our father again.

We found that if we piled the hay up by the loft window, we could sit on it and look out. Only hawks and buzzards, flying low over the pasture surrounded by trees, could be seen. I could not separate and define the feelings that arose in me as I looked out that window. I remember that I was afraid and I knew I would never come to accept life here.

Our quiet times in the loft ended in November when Benny found us there. We could hear him below—his coarse laughter echoing through the stables. Hurrying down the ladder, I heard Betty, who had reached the floor of the barn and had Carolyn by the hand, frantically yell, "Run, Anne."

Racing after my sisters, I glanced back once to see Benny behind me with a pitchfork held high over his head.

As we neared the house, Mrs. Coburn came out on the porch. Her hand went to her heart and her mouth opened. By the time we reached the porch, she had composed herself. "Now what did you do to annoy him?"

Betty had not released her hold on Carolyn. Out of breath and shaking, she said to Mrs. Coburn, "Nothing. We did nothing."

"Go to your room," Mrs. Coburn said. Then she walked slowly toward Benny who sat under a tree with the pitchfork lying across his lap and his head in his hands.

Mrs. Coburn's Bible reading was shorter and her prayer

was longer that evening. She begged the Almighty to help these children be more kind to Benny. And that night Carolyn wet her bed for the first time. I can still see her now as she stood before Mrs. Coburn, saying in a plaintive voice, "I'm sorry."

"Well, I didn't know I was going to have a baby to take care of—you ought to be ashamed of yourself, a six-year-old girl," she said to Carolyn. "There is only one cure for bedwetting, and that is no evening meal."

For the remainder of our stay here, Carolyn had only two soda crackers and a glass of milk at suppertime.

On Sunday all work was put aside, and with Mr. and Mrs. Coburn and Benny, we walked a short distance to a dark little church. Before the service began, Mrs. Coburn pushed us in front of her and announced to some of the other churchgoers that we were orphans and she was nursing us back to health. As people entered the church they gathered around us, shaking their heads and murmuring, "Poor children, lost in the world." And to Mrs. Coburn they said, "Bless you, sister."

I remember the musty smell of the church, the somber tone of the organ, and the triumphant look on Mrs. Coburn's face as she marched us to the front of the church and took her place beside Mr. Coburn, who had seated himself immediately upon entering.

The service began with a few "Amens" from the back of the church. After the singing of a hymn, some members began to stomp their feet and clap their hands. Soon there was shouting, arm-waving, and people lying prostrate on the floor. Mrs. Coburn, with great feeling, took part in all of it. Only Benny, Mr. Coburn, and my sisters and I remained seated. Betty kept her eyes on her hands, Carolyn cringed as the shouting grew louder, and I stared at the chaotic scene before us. Benny's eyes were fixed on the ceiling. Mr. Coburn read silently from his Bible, ignoring all that was going on around him.

Although we attended services there every Sunday thereafter, I never got used to it and came to dread those days. After the service we would spend the rest of the day at home in grim silence in honor of the Lord's Day. The house was hushed—only the crisp burning of the fire could be heard. On that day, after more lengthy Bible readings, bedtime came before sundown.

———

Mrs. Coburn took great pride in her baking, and her favorite pastime was making sticky buns. The house would at first smell of the sweet yeast dough rising. Later as they baked, the brown sugar and nut topping smelled like candy. On baking days my sisters and I paid special attention to our chores, for if they were not done properly, we could not have any buns.

One cold January day as the sticky buns were baking, we were sent outdoors to "soak up some winter sunshine" —part of Mrs. Coburn's remedy for making us well. I was always grateful when she said, "It's a bit too cold for Benny today." This meant we could play without being on the watch for him.

We kept an old piece of rope hanging inside the barn, and when we were alone we jumped rope. It kept us warm and it was a game we enjoyed. Betty was good at this, and if Carolyn and I tired of playing, she would wind the rope around her hands to make it the right length for turning by herself. Then she would keep on jumping and counting to see how far she could go without missing.

Occupied in our own world that day, we were startled to hear Mrs. Coburn shout, "Girls, come here this minute."

I despised her accusing tone of voice and the way she looked at us, as if always finding fault. Many times I had visions of hiding from her or pulling some terrible prank. But her giant frame and domineering nature kept me from doing anything.

"Which one of you sneaked inside and took the tray of buns?" she demanded.

"We haven't been inside," Betty replied.

"Don't lie to me, she said. "Benny can't eat sweets—it had to be you three."

She pushed us inside and ordered us to our room. We sat on our beds for a long time, wondering what was going on. We could hear her going from one room of the house to another, opening closets and calling, "Benny, where are you?"

At the parlor—a room that was unlocked only once a week while she cleaned it—there was a loud knocking, and I heard Mrs. Coburn say, "Are you in there, Benny?"

Then there was the sound of someone retching. "Mama, Mama, help me," came the voice of Benny from behind the locked door. "I can't open the door. You have the key," Mrs. Coburn said.

We heard a key being turned in the door. "Oh, my God, did you eat all of them?" she asked in disbelief.

"Yes, Mama," said Benny weakly.

"Get into bed while I call the doctor," she said.

The telephone was in the hall not far from our room, and we heard Mrs. Coburn nervously asking the doctor, "How much should I increase his medicine?"

Later I heard her tell her husband that Benny had had one of his attacks and would be in bed a few days. She did not mention the sticky buns that night. She served a light supper, told us Benny was ill, and that we were not to make any noise.

While Benny recuperated, Mrs. Coburn became more irritable. Nothing we did pleased her. Her Bible readings warned us of the devil and the fires that would consume us, and her prayers were for "this poor boy who is diseased of mind and body."

At night I would lie awake for a long time, trying to interpret her readings and prayers. Whispering to Betty, I said, "Benny sure did get sick from all those sticky buns, didn't he?"

"I think there is something wrong with him," she said.

"What?"

"I don't know, Anne, but don't ever bother him."

Our reprieve from Benny was short. Within a week he was out of bed, moving about in his slow-footed way. Grinning at us, he said, "I ate all the sticky buns and you didn't get any." His mother looked at him, scowling slightly. Then she looked at us and was about to say something when there was a knock at the door.

The only visitor since we had been there had been an old man selling wood. He had stopped one cold afternoon to ask Mrs. Coburn if she needed wood for her stove. "Why should I buy wood from you when I've got plenty on my property?" she had answered as she sent him on his way. I had felt sorry for him, with his gloves full of holes and the sole of his shoe come loose.

The knocking became insistent. My sisters and I stayed in the kitchen while Mrs. Coburn, followed by Benny, went to answer the door.

A girl's voice said, "Well, you sure took your time."

"I'm glad you came, Virginia," said Mrs. Coburn.

"When you called, you said he might be dying—he looks all right to me," said the girl.

"Say hello to your sister, Benny," said Mrs. Coburn.

"Don't touch me!" Virginia said.

The three of them came into the kitchen, and I saw that this girl was the one in the framed picture on the piano. She was more beautiful than her picture, with long, wavy brown hair, enormous expressive eyes, and a full mouth.

"These are the three little girls I told you about," said Mrs. Coburn. Turning to us, she proudly said, "This is my daughter, Virginia."

Benny, who had been sitting on his stool staring at Virginia, ran over to her, locked his arms around her neck and said, "I love you."

Virginia fought him off, and as he fell against the kitchen table, she screamed, "I said keep your hands off me!"

Mrs. Coburn told us to go to our room until supper was ready. I was glad to leave the kitchen. This beautiful girl had brought new unpleasantness to the house. In the kitchen the voices grew louder. My sisters and I listened and tried to understand.

"Now just settle down and let's enjoy your visit," Mrs. Coburn said.

"You got me here by saying Benny was sick, and he is not the least bit sick," said Virginia.

"Well, he was quite ill, but that was over a week ago. Why didn't you come sooner?"

"I have to go to school."

"Are you coming back home after you finish?"

"I told you I will never live in the same house with that dimwitted brother," Virginia shouted.

"I will not go through that with you again," said Mrs. Coburn. "The Lord would punish me the rest of my life if I had Benny put away like you suggested."

Then we heard the back door open, and Mr. Coburn came in. He welcomed his daughter home, and Virginia's voice became calm as she said, "Oh, Daddy, it's so good to see you."

We were called into the kitchen. After making her mother change places with her at the table so she would not have to sit by Benny, Virginia talked with her father. Occasionally she looked at Benny and said, "Would you please close your mouth when you eat."

Mrs. Coburn said little, and each time Benny started to speak, she put her hand on his arm and said, "Not now, Benny." She did not attempt to enter in the conversation with her husband and daughter, and she didn't seem to care that they excluded her.

Virginia left early the next morning, saying that if she walked a half mile up the road, she could catch the bus. Mrs. Coburn stood on the porch, looking wistfully after her until she disappeared around the bend. They had not kissed goodbye, but for a long moment had stood facing each other, their breaths steaming in the cold January air.

Winter dragged on. The floors were scrubbed, the laundry rubbed, the kitchen cleaned three times a day. We consumed quantities of the dark brown medicine and listened nightly to the Bible readings and prayers. On rainy afternoons when we could not go outdoors, we washed windows or took turns churning. I liked seeing butter form on top of the cream, but it was a long process and my arms hurt.

Only once was I put in the springhouse for punishment, and that was enough to keep me on guard against future misdeeds. While drying the dishes one day, a plate slipped from my hands and ended up in pieces on the floor. "Get your coat and come with me," Mrs. Coburn said, in that harrumph kind of way, as if she had been waiting for this moment. I followed her to the springhouse, unaware of what the next two hours would be like. Opening the small door, Mrs. Coburn said, "Go on in there, Anne, and think about what you have done."

The springhouse was a small, wooden shed built around a spring which was icy-cold year 'round. Here Mrs. Coburn kept her milk, butter, a white cheese she made herself, and leftover food. There were large crocks in one corner where kraut, cucumbers and beef marinated. The air was heavy and damp but strangely fresh. Tiny bits of sunlight found their way through cracks in the wood siding, otherwise there was darkness. There was no place to sit except on the cold earth floor. For two hours I paced that small area of darkness, wanting to scream, cry, and release the hatred inside of me. My memories of the past and hopes for the future disappeared in the frustration of my helplessness.

To celebrate my eighth birthday in February at the Coburn's, Betty said that I could choose the games we played outdoors. My sisters had made the day extra special by letting me sit on the chair while they scrubbed the floor of our room.

For March, Betty had circled two dates on her calendar. One was Carolyn's seventh birthday. The other was the anniversary of our mother's death.

We often reflected on our memories of her, but more and more our recollections were blurred by the remembrance of her funeral, the grave in the churchyard where we had stood together, and the events that had followed. There was no tangible evidence of our past and no guarantees for our future. Our one enjoyment in life lay in the belief that someday we would be reunited with our father.

For her seventh birthday, in March, Carolyn said she wanted to take a walk to the creek. We did not know the bounds of the Coburn property. In front of the house a long grassy area stretched to the road. To the right of the house was the springhouse, to the left the big grey barn. Just below the barn in a wooded section was a low rock wall, and on the other side, a creek about four feet wide.

We were sitting by the creek that March afternoon, tossing small stones in the water and trying to see if we could hit twigs floating here and there, when Benny suddenly appeared at the end of the wall. "You won't get away this time," he said. He grabbed Betty and pushed her to the ground. Betty kicked wildly, and Carolyn and I screamed, "Stop, Benny! Stop!" His maniacal laughter echoed through the woods as he held Betty's face in the water.

Carolyn and I picked up a large broken tree limb, and with all our force came down hard across Benny's back.

He let go of Betty and gave a piercing scream. A moment later his mother ran toward us down the hill. A cloud of dust rose behind her, and her wide mouth was set in anger.

Benny fell to the ground, crying, "Mama, Mama, they hurt me."

Carolyn and I sat beside Betty, wiping the muddy water from her face with our dresses while she choked and tried to get her breath.

"What did they do to you?" Mrs. Coburn asked Benny.

"My back, my back, they hit me with a tree."

Pulling up his shirt and seeing the swelling red line across his back, Mrs. Coburn shrieked, "Who did this?"

I took Carolyn by the hand and stepped closer to Mrs. Coburn. "We did it," I told her.

"He held Betty's face in the creek and tried to drown her," Carolyn said, and I was proud of her forcefulness.

"We hate him! We hate him!" I yelled at Mrs. Coburn. Without another word, she took Benny into the house.

That night I heard her tell Mr. Coburn, "We are going to have to send those girls away." When he asked why, she replied, "They are just too much trouble."

A week later our suitcases were packed, and once again we waited for the woman in black to come for us.

Mrs. Coburn made little effort to conceal her relief that we were leaving. But Benny cried when we left and ran behind the car, waving his arms and shouting, "Come back, chaps, come back!"

I felt a great weight lifted from my body that morning as the neat white house, the tragic mother, and her son disappeared behind me.

The past six months had been like years, and I was too weary to think about what might be ahead. I leaned back against the seat of the car, Betty and Carolyn beside me, and watched the fields and fences go by.

CHAPTER VI

~~~~~~~~~~~~~~~~~~~~~~~~~

March winds blew across the countryside. Tall bare trees bowed to the grey-brown earth, and dark clouds sailed across the sky. As I looked out the car window and stared up at the clouds, I felt that I too was floating in endless turbulence. Where would this journey take us, I wondered, looking at the woman in black who sat stiffly at the steering wheel. She held it tightly in white-gloved hands. Her black, narrow-brimmed hat was tilted perfectly to the right, and the letters on her pocket said, "Social Services." Who was this woman who knew where our father was and where we were going? Why did she not tell us?

Looking at my sisters beside me, I saw their frayed, brown coats and their pale despondent faces. We had come to confront each new move with resolute fear. Time had dimmed our hope of seeing our father again. The transient, inescapable madness of our lives brought only the challenge of survival—it was on this we were forced to center our attention. There was no need even to talk about it anymore.

I could feel the suitcase under my feet on the floor of the car. In the beginning my sisters and I had disliked these cardboard cases with the straps around them, but now they had become our treasure chests. I often looked at my possessions, especially Emily, and it was strangely comforting to feel the suitcase under my feet, because it represented the only constant in my disrupted life.

We had come to the outskirts of Charlotte and were going through some residential sections. I could hear the shouts of children as they played ball in a vacant lot; I saw ladies sorting vegetables at a stand in front of a grocery store; and I could smell the big city bus ahead of us. How busy and friendly it all seemed after our isolated life out in the country.

The woman in black drove slowly through a section of small houses with well-kept yards. Looking at the numbers on the houses, she said to herself as she stopped the car, "There it is."

Each time we had gone with the woman in black I felt panic when the car finally stopped at our destination. Fear in all its horrible shapes danced in my mind and I relived the strains of the past months. My terror mounted as we got out of the car.

Once again my sisters and I stood side by side with our suitcases, waiting for a door to open and an unfamiliar voice to say, "Come in." Though there was sadness in Betty's eyes, she squared her small shoulders as if to prepare for whatever was to be. Carolyn, with large fearful eyes, stood close to Betty.

The door opened, we stepped into the house, and a woman's cheerful voice said, "Hello, girls." She was not very tall, almost plump, and had soft, wavy brown hair. There was something about her expression, her gracious manner, her gestures, that possessed me immediately. I could feel the outer edges of my fear drop away as she smiled with her eyes. Her small mouth looked as if she could easily burst out laughing. It was easy for me to smile back at her.

"This is Mrs. Nye," said the woman in black. Then pointing to each of us in turn, she said, "This is Betty, Anne, and Carolyn."

Mrs. Nye took our coats and told us she was so glad to meet us.

"It is certainly a relief that you can keep them this week," said the woman in black.

"Oh, I don't mind," replied Mrs. Nye.

"Well, Mrs. Coburn was insistent that I pick them up today, and the home we had in mind can't take them for another week."

"They'll be just fine," Mrs. Nye said.

"Here are some notes on the girls and my telephone number. I'll see you next Saturday," said the woman in black as she made her usual hasty departure.

"Come with me, girls, and I'll show you my little girl," said Mrs. Nye, leading us through the dining room and into a bedroom.

Standing in a crib was a small child with gold hair. "This is Marilynn," said Mrs. Nye as she lifted the little girl out of the crib.

"How old is she?" asked Betty.

"She was a year old last month," Mrs. Nye replied.

"Can she walk?" I asked.

"Not too well, but she tries," Mrs. Nye said.

"Can we play with her?" asked Carolyn.

"Oh, yes, that would be a big help while I do a few things," she said as she took us into the dining room. Putting Marilynn down on a soft blue rug, Mrs. Nye said she thought it would be a good idea if first we all had some cookies and milk.

While we ate, she asked each of us what grade we were

in at school. Betty said that she had been in the second grade, and I had been in the first grade, but we had not gone to school this past year.

"Did you miss not going to school?" Mrs. Nye asked.

"Yes," said Betty, "very much."

"I didn't," I said.

"I wanted to be in first grade. I can already count and print my letters," Carolyn said.

"That's nice, how did you learn to do all that?" Mrs. Nye asked, smiling at Carolyn.

"Betty taught me in the barn," Carolyn answered.

Mrs. Nye looked briefly puzzled and did not ask any more questions.

We played with Marilynn. At first she crawled in and out from under the table, then Carolyn and I held her hands while she walked. We rolled a ball to her, she rolled it back. We tied her shoes, she untied them. We hid behind the door, she crawled over and found us.

Then I became aware of delicious smells coming from the kitchen, Mrs. Nye setting the table, and the darkness outside. A car came into the driveway, and Mrs. Nye said to Marilynn, "Here's Daddy!"

The tallest man I had ever seen came in. His eyes registered surprise at the trio of little girls he saw playing on the floor, and Mrs. Nye seemed a bit nervous. But before she could say anything her husband came over to us. His eyes flashed with humor as he put his hands on his hips, leaned slightly backward and said, "I'll tell you my name if you'll tell me yours."

We told him our names. "How do you do, ladies, I am Jennings Nye," he said.

Then he asked our ages. Betty said she was nine. I said I was eight. Carolyn said she was seven.

"You're a bunch of old ladies," he laughed as he threw

back his head. Then he picked Marilynn up and tossed her into the air, saying, "Wheee, wheee!"

Mrs. Nye gave her husband a relieved sort of smile and resumed her easy manner. She and her husband had some months before made application for "one girl" with the Mecklenburg County Children's Bureau. Just that morning the social services had telephoned to ask if she could take three girls who needed a home for a week. She had agreed without asking her husband, then spent the day wondering if this was right. Now she knew that it didn't matter.

We all sat down to dinner. At Carolyn's place were two soda crackers and a glass of milk. Mr. Nye said a simple blessing and began to serve our plates. Looking at Carolyn's plate, he asked, "Why does she have that?"

"The social worker told me she wets her bed if she eats supper," Mrs. Nye replied.

Mr. Nye ate quietly, glancing from time to time at Carolyn nibbling her crackers. Then he laid a piece of fried chicken on her plate, and when Mrs. Nye shook her head, he said, "The child needs to eat." While Carolyn ate the chicken, he put potatoes, green beans, and salad on her plate. Then he buttered a hot biscuit and as he gave it to her, leaned over and whispered, "If you want anymore, just ask for it." Carolyn's eyes lit up, and each night after that she raced to sit next to Mr. Nye, knowing that he would fill her plate.

In our bedroom there was a double bed for Betty and me, a single bed for Carolyn, a small chest of drawers, and a vanity. Mrs. Nye told us we could put our clothes in the chest if we wanted to, but we said no and put our suitcases under the bed, as we had always done. She helped us with our baths, stayed with us while we said our prayers, then tucked us in.

Mr. Nye stuck his head in. "Goodnight, ladies, sleep tight, and don't let the bedbugs bite."

"Don't pay any attention to him—he likes to tease," said Mrs. Nye as she turned out the light.

Talking in whispers, my sisters and I went over the day's transition. "I like it here," Betty said sleepily.

"She's being nice to us because we are only going to be here a week," I said.

"Where will we go next week?" Carolyn wondered.

"I'm just glad we left Mrs. Coburn," I said.

I wanted to erase from my mind all thoughts of Benny and Mrs. Coburn, but I knew they would be in my recollections forever.

By contrast, this house and these people who were going to keep us for a week had lifted my spirits. But a week was short—I must not give in to this temporary amenity.

The next morning I awoke to hear Mrs. Nye softly singing "Swanee River." Her pitch was not perfect, and she hummed words she could not remember. We got up, dressed, and joined her and Marilynn in the kitchen.

"How did you sleep, girls?" she asked as she fixed us breakfast. Then she had to do some laundry. Pulling out a big, white washing machine, she told us to get the clothes we had worn the day before. I couldn't wait to see how the machine operated and ran to get my clothes.

Mrs. Nye came into the room as I was going through my suitcase. She picked up one of my three cotton dresses, made in the state prison workshop. A look of distaste passed over her face, but she said nothing.

Kneeling on the floor going through my suitcase, I looked up to find her watching me.

"Is that your doll?" she asked.

"Yes, her name is Emily—she used to be pretty, but Benny got her dirty and now she isn't pretty," I replied.

Mrs. Nye picked Emily up and looked her over. "She isn't so bad—why don't we make her a bed where she'll be comfortable."

Speechless, I watched her go through the closet until she found a large shoe box. Then she took two small towels from the linen closet. Folding one neatly, she laid it in the box, placed Emily in the box and covered her with the other towel. Emily's feet protruded over the end of the box, but the grey face with the big red smile looked happy.

We went into the kitchen, where Mrs. Nye let us pull the lever that started and stopped the washing machine, and let us take turns putting the clothes through the wringer. How nice it was not to have to scrub on a washboard.

We spent the rest of the morning playing with Marilynn under the persimmon trees and investigating the yard. A lot on one side of the house was used for a small garden. The space on the other side was fenced, and there were several goats inside. Mrs. Nye said the goats belonged to some people nearby. There was a garage, with a room on one side for storage; a small fenced area with some chickens; and a large front yard with evergreens and newly planted trees. There was a birddog named "Trick" who followed us around, and a cat who preferred to keep her distance.

During the afternoon Mrs. Nye sewed buttons on our underwear, mended tears in our dresses, and talked to us. Betty asked if she could look through the books in the bookcase. Mrs. Nye's face lit up. "Of course," she said. Soon the two of them were discussing stories and authors

103

while Carolyn and I played on the floor with Marilynn. The afternoon passed in lazy contentment.

When Mr. Nye came home that evening, he rattled a bag behind his back and said with a mischievous grin, "O.K. girls, if you can guess which hand it's in, you can have it."

"That hand!" my sisters and I shouted at once.

Looking at his wife, Mr. Nye said, "Well, what do you know, Bernetta, they guessed it."

As he held the bag open for us to reach inside, I watched his eyes sparkle as each of us took out a B-B Bat. Not knowing how to react to his kindness, I looked away.

"Now where's your manners?" he asked.

"Thank you," said Betty as she nudged me to do the same.

In my room I unwrapped my lollipop, and took a few licks from it. It tasted so good I decided to put it in my suitcase because I might never get another, and I wanted to make this one last a long time.

I sat on my bed thinking about the tall, sandy-haired man who brought us the candy. In the evening when he came home from work, he put on a baseball cap and an old jacket and went outdoors. Trick was his dog and they loved each other—they had a language between them that only the two of them understood. While Mr. Nye worked about the yard or chopped wood, Trick was beside him and they conversed. Then they would go into the chicken yard to scatter the corn. Mr. Nye would stoop down and toss out small handfuls of the food. As the chickens came toward him, he talked to them. Between pecking at the corn, the chickens would make strange throaty noises back to him. I think it was then, as I listened to him communicate with the animals, that my first feeling for him became one of awe.

Although he was good-humored, he was not a frivolous man. His strength lay in his conviction that through hard work he would achieve what he wanted. Along the way he was prepared to laugh and give a great deal of himself to others.

Our week went quickly and pleasantly. Marilynn learned to say my name, she reached for my hand for support, and she hugged and kissed me while we played. She did not know nor care that I was an orphan. She refreshed my desolate heart.

Mrs. Nye liked to talk to us. Mostly she explained things: how she made the biscuit dough; how the persimmons would ripen and she would make pudding from them; or why the wind came from a certain direction. She liked to watch the sky and predict the weather. "See those clouds," she would say, "I believe we are going to have a northeaster by morning."

As each day passed I felt closer to the Nye family, and I began having conflicting feelings. I wanted to give in to my growing affection for them, but at the same time I was building a wall around my sisters and myself. We had moved too much. There was no duration or continuity to our relationships. The scars were beginning to show.

On Friday evening, Mrs. Nye sat on the bed folding our clothes as we packed our suitcases. "I don't know what time the lady will come for you tomorrow," she said.

Occasionally I looked up from my packing to find her giving us a steady, gentle look. She folded and refolded each dress; she got up to get a little book of stories that Betty had liked that she wanted her to have. She put new shoelaces in Carolyn's shoes and gave me an empty powder box I had admired. Throughout the week she had shown no curiosity about our past. She had accepted us as visitors to her home—it would have been wrong to pry.

Now on our last night she seemed disturbed, almost angry. Finally she asked, "When did your mother die?"

"Two years ago this month," said Betty.

"And how many places have you lived since then," she continued.

Betty sat down and counted them off on her fingers. "The Catholic Home, the Orphanage, the Stamens', the Coburns', and here—five places."

"Some day we are going back to live with our daddy," I added.

Mrs. Nye thought about this for a moment, then she said with a smile, "You know, I think Jennings is going to make popcorn this evening."

Mr. Nye let us watch him make the popcorn. Then he gave each of us a big bowl and said, "Go to it, ladies!" His good humor throughout the week had been infectious, his jokes outlandish, but to a child hysterically funny. "Why does the chicken cross the road?" he would ask. He pretended he took off Carolyn's nose and found it behind her ear. He had brought us comic books, then read them himself. Now as we sat around the kitchen table eating popcorn, he made no mention of this being our last night.

Saturday morning came, and my sisters and I waited for the woman in black. I was sad, but also annoyed with myself for allowing this feeling to develop. "Where do you think we will go?" I asked Betty.

"I don't know," she answered, as though she too did not want to think about it.

The day ended, the woman in black did not come. I was puzzled and relieved. Had she forgotten us? Would she come tomorrow?

That night after we got into bed, Betty asked Mrs. Nye why the woman had not come for us.

"I don't know—maybe she was too busy. There's nothing to worry about. Go to sleep now and don't think about it," Mrs. Nye said in her soft assured voice.

I lay awake for a long time, unable to control my apprehensions. My suitcase was packed, Emily was squushed in her shoebox with the lid on and a string tied around it. I was not supposed to be in this house, in this bed. I felt as if I were suspended in mid-air, with nothing to hold on to.

On Sunday morning Mr. Nye made flapjacks. He flipped them high in the air while he whistled bits of one song and another. Then he took us to Sunday school. When he got to the church, he took us to our classes, introduced us to the teacher and said, "The girls are staying with my wife and me for a short time." He did not call us orphans, and the children accepted us as visitors.

Two weeks passed, and still the woman in black did not come for us. One day I heard Mrs. Nye tell her husband that she had called the Social Services about some new clothes for us. They had agreed to put some things together, but Mr. Nye would have to pick them up.

When he returned that evening he did not have the clothes, and his voice was full of indignation. "I couldn't take those clothes, Bernetta," he said.

Looking baffled, she asked, "Why not?"

"They were awful, they smelled horrible, they were not even sewn together right."

"Next Sunday is Easter. All the little girls at church will have on their finest. I'll just have to make these girls something," she said, as if she were thinking aloud.

Mr. Nye had grown up in a large, happy family on a tobacco farm in the southeastern part of North Carolina. He had put himself through the State University, had met Bernetta Jervis at a basketball game, and married her shortly afterward. They had bought a small house in

Charlotte, where Mr. Nye had a job with a wholesale grocery distributor. Not yet thirty years old, they took life one step at a time, budgeting their money and making plans.

As they stood looking at my sisters and me, I sensed their concern for us. Mr. Nye handed his wife some money and said, "Get whatever they need."

The next morning Mrs. Nye asked, "While I do some shopping today, would you girls like to go to a movie?"

We were so excited. We jumped up and down, clapped our hands, and danced around the room. Before we left the house, she checked us over. I watched her eyes go from my stringy brown hair to my battered brown shoes. She studied each of us for a long time, as if she were silently making plans. Leaving Marilynn with a neighbor, she took Carolyn by the hand, and the four of us walked a mile to the city bus.

Sitting in the dark theater with my sisters, I thought of the times when my father had taken us to the movies. Somehow I did not want to remember that now. I wanted only to enjoy this day, to come out of the theater and find Mrs. Nye waiting for us—and most of all I wanted to go home with her.

After the movie, Mrs. Nye took us to the Walgreen's drug store. "What would you like, girls?" she asked as we settled into the booth. Pictured on the front of the menu were sundaes with mounds of whipped cream and big strawberries—inside were more photos of cake with thick chocolate, pies with scoops of ice cream, and an enormous boat-shaped concoction with ice cream, nuts, and a cherry on top. With eyes popping I said, "I want that one," pointing to the boat-shaped dessert.

"Why don't you read the names of the desserts," Mrs.

Nye said, "That way, when the waitress comes you can give her your order properly."

With full stomachs and light hearts, we waited for the Thrift Road bus to take us home. Soon other people joined us at the bus stop. The new feeling of being with people caused my sisters and me to draw closer to Mrs. Nye. Just before the bus arrived, I heard a young girl say to her companion, "Aren't they pitiful?" In our isolation at the Coburn's I had forgotten how I looked. Now the indignities of the past flashed through my mind, and I made a dreadful face at the girl.

Soon after we got home, Mrs. Nye took me into the bedroom I shared with my sisters. "Sit here on the vanity stool," she said, facing me to the mirror. "Now while I get supper started I want you to make your face look like it did this afternoon before we got on the bus." Without looking back, she left the room.

This struck me as an odd thing to do, but after a few minutes I screwed up my face and stuck out my tongue. It was the first time I had seen a reflection of my distorted face, and once was enough. Mrs. Nye returned shortly and told me to sit on the bed beside her. "You know, Anne, you didn't hurt that girl one bit this afternoon, but I think you can see what it does to you." This was the first time I was ashamed of my behavior.

The next week Mrs. Nye spent most days and nights at her sewing machine. Over the clatter I could hear her singing "Beautiful Dreamer." I liked the words of her songs, and sometimes when I was alone, I went into the storage room by the garage and sang the songs to myself.

By Friday the dresses were finished, and we tried them on while Mrs. Nye watched, pleased. The dresses were all alike, pink dotted-swiss with a tiny bit of lace at the neck, and woven through the lace was a pink velvet ribbon. She had made each of us a white organdy pinafore to go over the dresses. She tied the wide sash into a huge bow in back, while I ran my hands over the lace and smelled the crisp new fabric.

Mr. Nye came into the room and stood beside his wife. The two of them were watching us, and as I looked at them I shivered. I saw my mother's and father's faces and heard my mother saying quietly to my father, "Look, the girls have new dresses."

I suddenly wanted to take the dress off and scream. But looking down at the ruffles and lace, I felt my anger ebb as I heard Mrs. Nye say, "Tomorrow we'll get new white shoes to go with the dresses."

After supper that night Mr. Nye said, "O.K. ladies, time for a haircut." He convinced us we would look like movie stars when he finished. Betty was first to sit on the high stool. When the cutting was finished, soft pale blond curls gathered about her face. Carolyn's auburn hair, a heavy mass halfway down her back, became little ringlets, covering her head and falling across her forehead.

My dark blonde hair did not have the slightest curl. Mr. Nye cut it straight around, just below the ear, and when I looked in the mirror, I knew I did not look like a movie star.

On Easter Sunday morning we put on the pink dresses, white pinafores, and new white shoes. Mrs. Nye fussed over us, puffing up sleeves, tying sashes, and combing hair. Then she stood back and looked at us, frowning slightly at me. She left the room and returned with a pink velvet ribbon, which she pinned in my hair.

Turning to look in the mirror, I saw a well-scrubbed

girl dressed in ruffles and lace. She was unrecognizable to me, and I was frightened. I was losing my familiarity with the past, without having any clear idea of the present or the future.

CHAPTER VII

On the first bright, warm day of summer I found a friend named Peggy. Each morning she pressed her freckled nose against the back screened door and called to Mrs. Nye, "Can your girls come out and play?"

With her two brothers and my two sisters we climbed trees, slid down red clay hills, walked through damp weeds to pick blackberries, and after a summer rain, ran barefoot in the puddles. Under a big oak tree on the edge of the woods across the street we built a playhouse of sticks and boards. We wore Mrs. Nye's castoff dresses and high-heeled shoes and played with our dolls.

On rainy days we sat under the dining room table, cut out paper dolls, colored pictures, and played with Marilynn. And every Saturday evening Mr. Nye brought us the surprise brown bags of bubble gum, lollipops or other treats. Some I would eat after dinner, some I saved and put in my cardboard suitcase under my bed.

Although no one mentioned her, thoughts of the woman in black occasionally obscured my happiness. Once, when I asked Mrs. Nye if I could take my new clothes with me when I left, she gave me a long, even look. With eyes full of undefiled thought, she touched my shoulder and said, "Of course, Anne."

I had in our three months at the Nye's eaten several of the lollipops in my suitcase and replaced them with bubblegum wrappers, comic books, and a jar of Pond's handcream. Mrs. Nye had bought me a jar of my own because I loved the scent of the cream. Sometimes I would sit on the floor looking through my suitcase and feel terribly proud of all my possessions.

The shriveled red balloon in the corner of the suitcase brought back memories of my father—memories that were beginning to blur and confuse me. The walnut was still there, shrunken and odorless. I remembered the big tree in back of the Catholic Home where I had found it, and the pensive look on Sister Catherine's face as she said goodbye to us that day.

The picture of the Sonja Henie doll was still folded in the celluloid soap holder. Now and then I took the picture out and thought about Tom at the orphanage. I wanted to see him and share my new fortunes with him. There was the sack of marbles, a reminder of my first year in school. I could pick out the four that Bucky had given me. Thinking of him made me smile. There was the handkerchief with the rosebud in the corner, splotched with the tears on the day I had said goodbye to Emma, Sara Jane's necklace and Thad's pennies, gifts from the only real friends I had had. I wanted never to part with my possessions.

After two years of moving about and uncertainty, we found ourselves settling into a way of life at the Nye's. On most Saturdays my sisters and I went to the movies downtown while Mrs. Nye shopped. Then we met her at the drugstore for refreshments. Sometimes she took us through the shops and department stores just to look around, and we saw the first escalator in Charlotte at Efird's department store. The escalator went up to the mezzanine where there was a bathroom. Mrs. Nye always made this an early stop, with four little girls. That first ride on the escalator was a thrill for us all. Mrs. Nye rode it twice, then stood at the bottom as we went up, waved to her from the balcony, took the elevator down, and got back on the escalator. Her face reflected her pleasure in our enjoyment—until the store manager gave her a frown that sent us scurrying out of the store.

On Saturday nights, Mr. Nye would ask us to recite the Bible verse that was our lesson for the following day. On Sundays, Mrs. Nye always made sure that we were clean and well-dressed. After church we went home to a big Sunday dinner, and I ate enormous portions of everything. Then Mr. and Mrs. Nye often took us to the airport park, where there was a ferris wheel, merry-go-round, and ice cream cones. Carolyn especially loved the ice cream, and as we neared the park, she would lean over the seat and say to Mr. Nye, "I smell ice cream." He always insisted he didn't smell anything.

I think Mr. Nye enjoyed these outings as much as we did. He would lift each of us up on a merry-go-round horse, then stand beside Marilynn as we all rode round and round. To his wife's dismay, he bought us cotton candy and peanuts. He did not think of candy as causing tooth decay. To him such indulgence was something every child should experience.

His joys in life came from simple things—watermelon on a hot afternoon, fishing with his friends, raising a vegetable garden. I never heard him say a harsh word to or about anyone. If there was someone he did not care for, he simply avoided them in person and in conversation.

He had an indirect way of teaching us. During supper he would look at one of us and ask, "What is four times three?" Later, without warning, he would ask, "How do you spell Mississippi?" If we mispronounced a word, he would say, "Let me hear you spell that word." It didn't take me long to stop saying "becuz" and say "because."

Mr. Nye also had a way of disciplining us without saying a word. My friend Peggy and I always sat together in church, and Mr. Nye sat on the opposite side of the room. On one particular Sunday, Peggy and I were watching the woman in front of us, who wore a small blue hat with little flowers popping out all around it. As she sang, her jaw quivered and the flowers bounced up and down. A little rosebud finally came loose, and as it fell down the neck of her dress, she jumped and hit a high note where there was no high note. I stifled my giggles until I could bear it no more, finally laughing out loud. Mr. Nye walked all the way around the back of the church and with everyone looking on, took his place between Peggy and me. I was humiliated, not because of what the people would think, but because Mr. Nye had caught me in such bad behavior. I was sure he would tell Mrs. Nye and I would be punished, but he never mentioned it.

Each morning that summer I awoke with only the thought of playing with my sisters and friends. One day, however, Mrs. Nye sat down at the breakfast table with a serious look. "Girls," she said, "I think we are going to have to make some rules around here." This was to be the beginning of a regimen of discipline for which I was unprepared.

"There will be plenty of time to play," she said, tracing a design in the tablecloth with her finger, "but you will never amount to anything if you do not do something worthwhile each day."

She had drawn up a chart that gave each of us two

chores a week. Whoever did her job the best each week would be rewarded with a prize. Then her voice became more grave. "I do not like the idea that you have missed a year of school. I have a teaching degree, and I have checked with the board of education about teaching you this summer. If you pass the test that the board will give you at the end of the summer, you can go into your proper grade in the fall."

We had fallen behind a year in school during the time we had been at the Coburn's. If we could catch up, Betty would go into the fourth grade, I would go into the third, and Carolyn into the second.

The next day Mrs. Nye took us on the first of many trips to the library. She also belonged to several book clubs, and often told us about a book she was reading or read to us. The story I asked her to read again and again was "Peter Rabbit." It is to this day my favorite.

After we began going to the library, we had to read to her. "Enunciate your words, Anne—pause when you reach the end of your sentence," I can hear her saying. Sometimes she let us read silently and then tell her the story. An interval full of "and-ahs" meant we had to read the book again.

The first week our chores began. The chart said that I was to make the beds and feed the chickens. The bed-making went fine, but twice in that week I left the gate to the chicken yard open and the chickens got out. It took quite a bit of Mrs. Nye's time and patience to get them all back in again.

The first time I left the gate open, she scolded me and said I must pay closer attention to my chores. The second time she asked, "How could you forget to close the gate again?"

"I can't remember it," I replied.

"Don't say 'I can't,' because you can," she said emphatically. Then she added, "Go get me a switch, Anne."

Startled, I broke off a small branch from the nearest tree, handed it to her, and watched while she silently stripped the leaves off it. Her silence made me aware of her stern intentions. Then she held me by the arm and gave me three sharp licks on the legs. I ran crying to my room.

That evening she took me into her room and asked, "Anne, do you know why I punished you today?"

My feelings were hurt, my legs still stung, and I did not want to talk about it. Acting as if I didn't care, I said, "Yes."

"You must keep your mind on your work. Forgetting to close the gate once wasn't so bad, but the second time told me you had not learned anything. Maybe the switching will help you to remember," Mrs. Nye said in a low voice, as if she did not want to share this with anyone but me.

When the package arrived from the board of education, our studies began. Each day after lunch we sat around the dining room table while Mrs. Nye drilled us in spelling, math, and reading. Sometimes Peggy sat on the back steps waiting for me, sometimes she waited in our playhouse down by the woods.

"What's the matter?" Mrs. Nye asked when she saw me drawing circles on my math paper.

"I can't do it," I said.

"Don't say 'I can't' until you have tried," she said in the uncompromising tone she used at times like this. She showed me how to add three columns of numbers, and when I finished, said, "Good work, Anne."

Betty liked to study and did all her assignments to perfection. She learned cursive writing that summer, turning out pages of beautiful letters. I don't believe she ever missed a spelling word, and she read much further in her books than was assigned.

Carolyn was quick to learn. She was left-handed and was frustrated when her letters were illegible. But she soon found her own way with pencil and paper and did excellent work. In the short time we had been here, Carolyn had developed independence. Her cheeks were rosy, the lost and solemn expression was disappearing. Mrs. Nye gave her light chores to do and made her nap each afternoon.

As the summer went on, Mrs. Nye began to ask us about our family. She seemed especially interested in Aunt Carrie, my mother's sister, and one day asked if we would like to visit her. We agreed, and it was arranged that we were to go the following Saturday. Mr. Nye would drive us there, then pick us up. As we left, Mrs. Nye said, "Enjoy your visit, girls, and mind your manners."

During the half-hour drive we wondered what it would be like to see Aunt Carrie again. As we neared her house, I could smell fresh bread from the bakery a few blocks away. I had loved that smell when I passed the bakery with my mother and father. Now the yeasty bread and the familiar landmarks along the way were oppressive. I thought of the day so long ago when the woman in black had come and taken us away. I had wanted to see my Aunt Carrie then, but now I was not so sure.

When we entered the house, I could almost feel my mother's presence. There was the chair where she had sat. Beyond the living room was the breakfast room, where my mother and Aunt Carrie drank coffee while we played with Bobby, her son.

Aunt Carrie was glad to see us—maybe to ease her conscience that we were all right, maybe to recall again her sister's death. After she had hugged us, Uncle Charlie had pinched our full cheeks, and they both said, "My, how they have grown," there was a long, awkward silence.

At one time I had been comfortable here. I knew where Aunt Carrie kept her cookies and where Bobby's toy soldiers were. But I was uneasy as I sat rigid on the dark, prickly sofa, listening to Aunt Carrie ask, "Do you girls remember your mother?" She went into her bedroom and returned with a small framed picture of our mother. As we looked at it, I could hear Aunt Carrie saying, "Do you remember the funeral, girls?" "Do you remember how your mother used to bring you here for visits? Do you remember when Bobby broke his arm?"

Of course we remembered it all, and so much more. But I was too absorbed in my mother's picture to listen or to answer her questions. Looking at the photograph, I realized that the sadness of my mother's death would always be with me, but I had long ago accepted the finality of her being gone. I wanted my father. He was alive, and he had promised to come for us.

"Where is our daddy?" I asked.

"Oh, he has another job and a room in town. He often comes over for Sunday dinner. I'll have to tell him how well you girls look," she said.

The afternoon dragged by, and I watched out the window for Mr. Nye. After Aunt Carrie had talked about our mother, shown us the picture, and given us chocolate milk, she seemed at a loss as to what to do next.

When Mr. Nye came, Aunt Carrie put the picture of our mother back in her room, walked to the door with us, and our visit ended without her ever asking where these little girls she had known so well had been for the past two years.

Betty celebrated her tenth birthday that July with a big chocolate cake with ten candles. As she closed her eyes to make a wish before blowing out the candles, I sensed the seriousness of her mood. She had borne her grief and tribulations with gallantry. If she had ever given in to her unhappiness, she had done so in private. She was the center of my life. As Mr. Nye sang "Happy Birthday," I looked at her and knew that whatever her wish might be, at this moment she was happy.

Just after the birthday—and scarcely two weeks after our visit to Aunt Carrie—Mrs. Nye told us that our father had called to say that he was coming to see us.

I lay awake for a long time that night, trying to imagine what it would be like to see him again. I tried to visualize his face but could not. I thought I heard fragments of his voice, but that would vanish. I was frightened at being unable to bring into focus the face of the person that I loved the most.

When our father came the next day, I did not run to him as I had thought I would. Instead I stared at his sea-blue eyes, his graying hair, and the broad shoulders where I had once loved to sit. How familiar he looked, and yet like a stranger.

I stiffened when he gathered us in his arms and called us "my babies." Betty said, "Hello Daddy" and sat in a chair across from him. Carolyn remained on his lap while he took some chewing gum from his shirt pocket and gave each of us a piece.

He made no apologies for his long absence, he asked no questions about where we had been. He commented on our growth, but I knew he still saw us as babies. He called me Annie Laurie, but he did not sing to me—and I did not ask him to.

All the dreams I had had of seeing my father again came together in this one moment, but now I was confused.

When situations had seemed unbearable during the past

two years, I had found comfort in thinking about my father. I had envisioned myself running into his arms and hearing him say, "I've come to take you home." I knew now, at age eight, that I would never have those dreams again. I thought I would choke from the lump in my throat.

My father came to see us several times during the rest of that summer. Sometimes he appeared without warning, calling to us as we played outdoors. There were times when he brought us small gifts, and there were times when he seemed to come without really knowing why. Our conversations were strained, and for days after each visit I was tortured by feelings of guilt. Then as abruptly as his visits began, they ended.

I don't recall when Mrs. Nye suggested we call her "Mother." She had left the decision up to us, but said she thought it might help Marilynn learn to say the word more quickly if we used it. "But you must never forget your own mother," she added.

She also began to introduce us to people as "my girls," never saying the first three are orphans and the youngest one is mine. Quite often people would remark about how much Carolyn resembled her. Mrs. Nye's eyes would light up, and there would be her shy smile. I liked people thinking of me as her daughter, but I was not yet ready to call her Mother.

Mrs. Nye became increasingly occupied with our manners and behavior. Punishment for offenses ranged from an afternoon in your room while the other children played to writing an apology one hundred times.

The reward for a job well done might be a little extra money for Saturday shopping or a new dress. The reward

I cherished most was a navy-blue linen purse with white daisies embroidered on it. Mrs. Nye had seen me admire it in a store window. "Do you like that purse?" she asked, one woman to another.

"Oh, yes, I think it is the most beautiful one I've ever seen," I answered.

"It is rather nice," she said.

I thought about the purse during the next week but not enough, for no matter what chore I was given, I either looked for a quick way out or I shunned it.

Washing dishes was my least favorite job—the pots and pans being my worst enemy. If food was stuck on them, I did a bit of scraping, and what didn't come off remained on the pan as I dried it and put it away.

When Mrs. Nye found the dirty pan, she asked, "Why did you put this away dirty?"

"I can't get it clean," I answered.

"Now don't say 'I can't'," she would say. Then she would pull out all the pans and I would start over again.

After three nights of inspecting my pots and finding them in need of further scrubbing, she said to me, "Anne, I guess you had better stay home Saturday morning and help me in the garden while the other girls go to the movies."

I had not expected a reward that week, but to miss the movie was dreadful. Saturday I did the gardening, and I made a special effort the following week to do all my chores carefully. Toward the end of the week Mrs. Nye asked me to come into the garden with her. Handing me the shears, she said, "Mrs. Russell is having company for dinner and she would like a nice centerpiece. I'm going to let you fix it for her."

I knew the pride Mrs. Nye took in her arrangements, and couldn't believe she was asking me to do this. After I had selected the flowers, she got out a vase. Other than offering a bit of advice like, "make sure the tall ones are in the center, and mix the ferns as you go along," she left me to do the job.

When I had finished, she admired my work profusely, then said, "Take it over to Mrs. Russell and tell her you did it all by yourself." As I went down the back step, she came to the door and called out, "You might tell her that you helped grow them as well." I was full of pride as I walked next door with my first bouquet of flowers.

When I returned, Mrs. Nye said, "Anne, there is something for you on your bed." I was not used to surprises from her. If she made a promise, she kept it, no matter the cost or inconvenience to herself. If she said "No" to a request, I always knew there was no point in pursuing it further. She never deviated from this.

There on my bed, in a little white box from Ivey's department store, was the navy-blue purse with the white daisies. I wanted to run to her, throw my arms around her, and thank her but I resisted the urge. Looking up, I saw her standing in the doorway, her face mirroring the happiness she derived from my pleasure.

"Thank you," was all I could say.

"You earned it," she said, to let me know that the gift was not given out of folly.

———————

By late summer her flower garden had become a large part of my life. It had been Mrs. Nye's last resort as a means of punishing me, or at least that was my thinking at the time. I know now that discipline was only part of her motive. She switched me for going to Peggy's house without permission; she switched me for being insolent; and she switched me for saying I had done my reading when I had not. None of this seemed to work. Finally, after pacing the floor and calling me headstrong, she had taken a different approach. "You will have to spend the mornings working in the garden." she said, as if this would solve everything.

For the rest of the summer I pulled weeds by the hundreds and helped bring many loads of mulch from the woods across the street. Wearing her big straw hat, Mrs. Nye would get out the wheelbarrow, put Marilynn in it, and the three of us would go into the woods. At first I was anxious to get the job over with, but Mrs. Nye liked to walk along slowly, singing her Stephen Foster songs.

Once in the shade of the woods, she would lean against a tree, holding her rake and fanning herself with her hat. She liked to look around and enjoy the quiet beauty. Sometimes she would say, "Look, Anne, there are some rabbit tracks." Another time she would tell me the names of the birds from the sounds they made.

While she raked the mulch into piles, I put Marilynn in the wheelbarrow and gave her rides. I had developed a special feeling for Marilynn. At first it was protectiveness because she was only a year old. Then it became a feeling of comradery. I liked being with her. She tried to imitate everything my sisters and I did, and we had taught her to say big words like Constantinople and Ecclesiastes. On Saturday mornings she listened to the "Let's Pretend" program on the radio with us, and afterwards Betty would read Marilynn the fairy tale that had been done on the show.

As Mrs. Nye and I piled the mulch into the wheelbarrow, she sometimes studied me. Once she asked, "How would you like some new glasses before school starts?"

"O.K.," I replied, without much interest.

"You know glasses can be attractive on some people," she continued.

"I hate them."

"What else do you hate?"

Without hesitating, I told her I hated my teeth and my straight hair.

"Well, Anne, a person's looks reminds me of those pots and pans you have been having so much trouble with lately. You know the pan can be shiny and pretty on the outside, but if the inside is dirty, it is of no use to anybody. That's true of people, too—people can be beautiful, but filled with hostility and ugliness on the inside, they are useless people."

She would end her conversation there, without further definition. As we picked Queen Anne's lace along the way returning to the house, I would think about what she had said. Later she would show me how to dip the flowers in different colors of ink to make a varied bouquet. Then she would add one last thought for the day, "There, Anne, you see it takes all the colors to make a nice bouquet—some of them are not as pretty as the others but I don't see them slumping over, feeling sorry for themselves."

Though I could not admit it to her then, I learned to love the feel of the earth and seeing buds open into blossoms. There was satisfaction in the beauty of her garden. But most of all I came to like our times together in the woods.

For a while I viewed with absolute amazement Mrs. Nye's method of detecting when we didn't tell the truth. The first time she performed the fingerprint test on us was a steamy day in late July, and she had just scrubbed and waxed the kitchen floor. My sisters and I were outdoors when she called to us, "Don't come inside 'till the floor dries."

It wasn't long before I wanted a drink of water, and forgetting her warning, walked across the sticky floor.

"Who did this?" asked Mrs. Nye when she saw the tracks.

"Not me," my sisters and I said at once.

"Well, I guess I'll just have to do the FBI test to see who is telling the truth," she said, getting out the black iron skillet Mr. Nye used for pancakes. We lined up in front of her while she pressed each of our thumbs onto the skillet and then onto a piece of paper. Then she told us to go into the other room while she studied the prints.

After a few minutes, she called us back and said, "Well, Anne, the test shows that you are the guilty one."

Her accuracy scared me. I never challenged her method, and for a while thought she might be an agent for the FBI. It was years before I realized that it was my face and not my fingerprints she studied.

————

After my chores were finished one day, I asked permission to go to Peggy's house. With a sigh, Mrs. Nye said, "You may go, but you must be back in one hour because I want to call out your spelling words to you before suppertime."

I went to Peggy's house, and returned as the table was being set for supper—at least three hours later than I had promised.

Trying to control her exasperation, Mrs. Nye said, "After supper, Anne, you can write each of your spelling words fifty times."

I simmered with anger throughout the meal. Then I made my decision. I would run away.

Cleaning the dishes off the table, Mrs. Nye said, "Now get your paper and pencil and get busy."

With all the defiance and false courage I could muster, I said, "I'm leaving."

She gave me a quick, startled look. "Well, Anne, let me pack you a few things to eat—you may get hungry along the way."

I was stunned by her reaction, but determined to carry through with my plans. My sisters looked at me in disbelief while Mrs. Nye put two apples, some cheese and crackers into a small box, handed it to me and said, "Take care of yourself, Anne."

It was dark and still outside. I could hear the crickets and smell the soft dewy haze of the summer night. Looking into the long stretch of blackness ahead of me, I became petrified. I walked about two blocks away from the house and sat down on the curb. As I took out one of the apples and began to eat it, I heard footsteps coming toward me. I was numb with fear as I watched, through the dim streetlight, the figure of a man approach. "What are you doing here, child?" he asked in a surprised voice.

I grabbed my box of food and ran toward home. When I reached the back door, I found it locked. I knocked softly, and almost instantly the door was opened by Mrs. Nye, "Well, look who has come to visit us!" she exclaimed. My sisters ran to greet me with a mixture of relief and weariness at my behavior.

After everyone else had gone to bed, Mrs. Nye poured me a glass of milk, and she and I stayed at the kitchen table. For a few minutes she sat quietly, smoothing the folds of her dress. Then she said, her manner showing the difficulty she had expressing these things, "I'm glad you came back, Anne."

I wanted to apologize, but the words would not come. I

looked at her face and saw the twinkle, even now, behind the sadness in her eyes. The sensation that I might some-day be taken from her filled me with remorse for my behavior. It was then that I knew how much I wanted to live with her. I put my head in my arms on the table and cried. She patted me gently on the shoulder. "Tomorrow will be a better day."

I knew summer was about to end when the test papers arrived from the board of education. Mrs. Nye looked through them carefully, and then at my sisters and me sitting nervously at the table. "We have a week before we must return them," she said. Then she laid the papers aside and said, "I suggest we go to the county fair today."

She was as excited as we, riding on the bus that would take us to the fairgrounds. When we arrived at the gate, we held Marilynn's hands while Mrs. Nye bought the tickets. The smell of popcorn and hotdogs filled the air, and as far as I could see were booths with jams, jellies, cakes, and crafts. I had never seen anything like this and my heart pounded with excitement.

We had not gone far onto the grounds when a man approached us, holding aloft a handful of balloons. "How about a balloon for the little girls?" he shouted above the noise of the fair.

"Why, thank you," said Mrs. Nye.

"How many children do you have?" he asked as he began to separate the strings of the balloons.

"Four," she said without hesitation.

He handed each of us a balloon. Mrs. Nye thanked him again, and we started to walk away.

"Wait a minute, lady," he snarled at us. "What makes

you think them balloons is free? You owe me forty cents. Gimmie the money."

I snatched the balloons from my sisters, and with my hand balled into a fist, hit him square in the stomach while the balloons bobbed against his face. "Take your damn balloons!" I screamed.

As the man staggered backward, Mrs. Nye hurried us away. When we had gotten a safe distance from him, she asked my sisters to watch Marilynn while she had a few words with me.

For one moment I thought I saw an impish look cross her face. Then in a stern voice she asked, "Anne, I want to know, where did you hear such a horrible word?"

"I don't know—I think when I went to school," I answered, not fully realizing what I might have said.

"You must never let me hear you say that again," she said.

Then she told me the man was right, that she should have known better. "He probably has a family to feed," she said with such sympathy and feeling that for a moment I thought she was going back to buy the balloons.

On impulse I had felt a desire to protect this kind woman from the remarks of that rude man. How proudly she had told him she had four children. Maybe it was here, as I walked beside her through the crowds, that I had my first sense of really belonging.

Mr. Nye had harvested his vegetable garden, and only the late bloomers remained in Mrs. Nye's flower beds when she announced one morning that it would be a good day to start her fall house cleaning. She began taking down all the curtains, washing and starching them, and pinning them on wooden frames to dry. She told us we could do some cleaning in our room. I cleaned windowsills while Betty washed baseboards and Carolyn polished the furniture with lemon oil.

I had, in six months at the Nye's, come to love this room I shared with my sisters. The four-poster bed where Betty and I slept, the vanity with the wide mirror where I had made my last ugly face, the chest of drawers that stood empty—since our belongings were still in the suitcases under the bed—and the closet with all the pretty clothes Mrs. Nye had either bought or made for us. The shelves of the closet were stacked with comic books Mr. Nye had brought us, and on the floor of the closet were paper dolls, crayons, Chinese checkers, jacks, and games. I kept Emily in her shoebox beside my bed. She looked rather grand, I thought, wearing a pink baby dress that had once belonged to Marilynn.

My sisters and I were busy cleaning our room when Mrs. Nye called us outdoors. We followed her to the back of the garage, where she had a fire going in the big metal incinerator. On the ground beside it were our cardboard suitcases.

Without saying a word, Mrs. Nye picked one up and plunged it into the flames. I took a step forward, but stopped when I felt Betty's hand on my arm. Looking at my sister, I saw a questioning look dissolve into a small, set smile. The color drained from Carolyn's face as she reached for Betty's hand. Then the three of us watched in stunned silence as Mrs. Nye poked the suitcase down into the fire.

After a few minutes she put the second suitcase into the flaming barrel. Stepping back from the heat and wiping her forehead with the back of her hand, she glanced at my sisters and me. There was a look of satisfaction in her eyes, determination to her movements as she reached for the last suitcase. Just before placing it in the fire, she stopped and gave us a long unwavering look. There was again that light in her eyes, as the yellow glow of the flames brightened her face.

My sisters and I stood still until the suitcases had disappeared in the last sulky glow of the fire. Then Mrs. Nye walked toward us, and in a quiet voice said, "Shall we go back in the house now, girls?"

I went into our room and looked under the bed where our suitcases had been. What would I do when I had to travel again, I wondered. Then I thought about my treasures. Quickly I got up and looked in the chest.

Opening the top drawer I saw Betty's things. The middle drawer was mine—there were my clothes from the suitcase folded neatly at one side. On the other side were all my keepsakes except the walnut and the candy. They were gone. In the bottom drawer were Carolyn's things, among them a tattered little book Betty had given her called "Animal ABCs."

How nice everything looked in the drawers, I thought. And then remembering my suitcase, I had a tinge of guilt, as if I had abandoned a friend who had been with me for almost three years.

Just before the sun set that evening, I went alone to the incinerator for one last look. I saw only the charred metal buckles from the suitcase straps in the heap of ashes. Mrs. Nye came up behind me. "Anne," she said, "I'm sorry about the walnut and the candy, but you shouldn't keep such things in with your clothes." That was the only remark she ever made that was in any way connected with her burning the suitcases.

Late into the night I lay awake, thinking about what Mrs. Nye had done that day. I was first inclined to mourn the destruction of my suitcase, but at the same time I was relieved. Just before I fell asleep, my thoughts strayed from the lost suitcase. I felt somehow secure in the present, and I began to have a sense of my future.

It was a few days after the suitcases were burned that I called Mrs. Nye "Mother" for the first time. I remember she was standing at the kitchen sink with her back to me, and without any forethought I had asked, "Mother, can I go out now?"

She turned quickly, gave me a big smile, and said, "Anne." I realized what I had said and smiled back.

Then she picked up a towel and dried her hands. "The correct way to ask that question is 'May I go out?'—'Can I' implies, are you able?" I repeated the question and permission was granted.

I was astonished at how easily it happened. The word had come spontaneously, and I did not feel disloyalty to my real mother. I had thought about her every day since her death—always with a sense of depression and emptiness—and there would forever be a special place she would occupy in my thoughts. But time had brought about changes. I wanted and needed a mother.

Calling Mr. Nye "Daddy" also came naturally. Mother would say, "Go tell Daddy that supper is ready." I did not compare him to my father nor did I feel unfaithful. But somewhere I had crossed the line that separated my father from the rest of the world. He was part of a past that had begun to recede. And I wanted once more to see him, to ask his forgiveness for that.

We helped Daddy clean the cornstalks from his garden while Mother canned jars of vegetable soup. Then the first day of school arrived. Mother had been so proud of my sisters and me when we passed the board of education examination. Betty and Carolyn were excited about school, and even I managed some enthusiasm with my new eyeglasses, a reindeer sweater and some pleated skirts.

For an instant I felt panic as I boarded the big yellow bus for school that first day. There were rows of seats beneath the windows on both sides of the bus, called the side seats. Running the length of the middle of the bus was a long, low seat where children sat back to back, called the center seat. Only high school students were allowed to sit on the side seats, and the younger children in the center. My sisters and I sat close together on this center seat.

We each had a new book bag with a strap that went over the shoulder. In the bag were the new pencils and notebooks Daddy had bought us. Every now and then, Carolyn took out one of the pencils and admired it. Red was her favorite color, and Mother had bought her a dress with a bright red bodice and a red-checked skirt for her first day of school.

Betty whispered to me to be sure to get back to the bus on time at the end of the day. After we reached the school and the principal had told us where our rooms were, Betty said, "Please don't fight, Anne." Then she took Carolyn by the hand and disappeared down the hallway.

I was a new girl to the third grade, nothing more. And after Mother's careful inspection that morning, I was probably the cleanest girl in the school. I was no longer an orphan. I reveled in my new role.

One week passed without incident. Then I had my first confrontation with Jack O'Neil. He was sturdily built and full of bluster, while his twin brother Jerry was small and reticent. Both were in the third grade with me. I had seen

Jack bully other children, and I tried to keep my distance from him.

As the bus headed home that day, Jack was sitting with his back to mine on the center seats. Suddenly, he gave a hard push, and I landed on the floor under the side seat. As I got up and saw the malicious look on his face, I became wild with anger. Holding my book bag by its strap, I slung it at him. It hit him hard on the shoulder, he let out a yell and came at me across the seat. All I remember before the bus stopped were the voices of my sisters saying, "Anne, stop!"

I looked up to see the bus driver standing over me. "O.K., if you two want to fight, get off my bus," he said, motioning us toward the door.

We were a good three miles from home, and I was terrified at being left alone with Jack. To my relief he struck out in a run, turning only once to shout back at me, "I'll get even with you, four-eyes."

It took me a long time to get home that day, and I was filled with shame when I walked into the kitchen and saw the look on Mother's face. The beautiful dress she had made for me was torn halfway down the side. The sash was dragging on the floor. My lip was bleeding and I hurt all over. Full of disappointment, Mother said, "Go to your room, Anne."

I could hear the sounds of dinner being prepared and heard Daddy come home. My room had grown dark as I lay on the bed thinking. I had embarrassed my sisters on the bus, but I could not explain to them the humiliation of being pushed off my seat. Betty wore her dignity and calm as a soldier carries a shield—nothing, it seemed, could touch her. Carolyn's frail beauty and demure manner caused people to protect her. No, I thought, I cannot explain to them, when I have none of their qualities.

Mother came to the room with my supper on a tray, maybe to spare me the distress of facing the family, or maybe to punish me. For a while she sat quietly on the vanity stool as I ate. Then she asked, "Are you all right, Anne?"

"I guess so," I said, without looking at her. I knew she had already questioned my sisters about the fight, and there was no need for me to talk about it.

She examined me closely, put some mercurochrome on a cut on my chin, and told me to go to bed. Before she turned out the light, she said, "Let that be the end of your fighting."

But it was not. Jack continued to provoke me. And unfortunately, I had become his target. He hit, pushed, and punched every day. For each offense I slammed my book bag down on him. I didn't forget that Bucky had taught me to fight with my fists, but I couldn't fight Jack this way. He was more apt to grab my hair and pull me to the ground, or trip me so that I fell. Face-to-face fighting was not his style.

One November day, I was in line with the other children to board the bus to go home. With no warning, Jack gave me a mighty push that sent me crashing into his sister. She caught Jack and slapped him hard on his cheek. "You idiot!" she yelled at him while the other children stared.

I saw tears in Jack's eyes and a red hand-print on his face as he got on the bus. He sat quietly, holding his chin tight against his chest all the way home. I was surprised to see that, without rage and abuse, he was just an ordinary boy. Stealing glances, I felt a hint of sadness for him.

When I told Mother about the incident, she said, "Anne, you know Jack's mother is dead, don't you?"

Startled, I answered, "No, I did not."

"She died a few years ago. His father has a hard time trying to keep the family together. His sister had to take over the house and the younger children, which hasn't been easy for her."

I listened without saying a word as Mother went on, "Not long after Jack's mother died, his older brother was killed in a bus accident. Jack has a lot to be angry about right now, but someday he will get it all out, and then he'll be all right."

Jack and I continued to spar, but we never actually struck each other again.

Christmas was three weeks away when Daddy came home, smiling a certain way, with a large bag. After supper, he placed the bag on the table and took out a box of Christmas tree lights. "I think we ought to test these, don't you?" he said to his wife.

When the lights were plugged in and the room filled with color, I looked across the table at Mother. Her eyes were shining as she watched our faces.

The weeks that followed were filled with activity. My sisters and I shelled nuts for Mother's fruitcakes; we shopped for gifts for the family, carefully hiding them so everyone would be surprised on Christmas morning; and Daddy took us around Charlotte to see the lights and decorations.

A few days before Christmas, Daddy went into the woods across the street and chopped down a six-foot tree. He put the lights on it and let us help in the decorating. Then he held Marilynn up to put the star on top. When all was finished, he made us close our eyes before he turned the lights on. "No peeking now," he said. Then with great ceremony he counted, "One, two, three, ready!" Mother joined us in exclaiming over our beautiful tree.

Christmas morning came, and after breakfast we went into the living room. The night before my sisters and I had put our gifts for the family under the tree. Now there were more gifts, and the stockings Mother had bought for us were bulging.

Betty, Carolyn, Marilynn, and I sat on the floor while Mother and Daddy sat on the sofa. In a soft voice and with all traces of humor gone from his face, Daddy read from the Bible the story of Jesus' birth. He occasionally looked at my sisters and me. As he read this story, the parts of him fell into place for me. I could not then define him in words, but I know now that I saw him as the embodiment of justice and goodness.

After the reading we stayed on the floor while Daddy gave out the gifts. Our stockings were filled with candy, fruit, and nuts. I opened my little gifts first. A tapestry change purse from Betty, because I always lost my movie money; a card with four hair barretts from Carolyn; and a box of Gemey bath powder from Marilynn. This was Mother's favorite powder—I often asked to use hers.

I had waited last to open my largest gift, a beautifully wrapped box with a card that said, "For Anne—from Mother and Daddy." I could not imagine what was in it. I opened the lid and gasped with surprise—there was the Sonja Henie doll. She wore a short red dress, and had little white skates. Tiny flowers were pinned in her long blonde hair. Her eyes opened and closed. I looked at her for a long time in disbelief, and then I looked at Mother. I did not have to ask how she knew that I had wanted this doll all my life. As I studied Mother's face, I wanted to frame it and keep it forever in my memory.

I looked around at the shimmering tree and at Daddy sitting on the floor with Marilynn. The house smelled of pine boughs Mother had used in decorating and turkey roasting in the oven for our Christmas dinner. But it was not for this that my thoughts gave way to wonder. It was seeing the light in Carolyn's eyes, the copper curls bouncing as she danced around the room. It was seeing the peace on Betty's face, and the shoulders that no longer sagged with her burdens.

When the excitement of Christmas morning had passed, I took the Sonja Henie doll back into our room and laid her down beside Emily, the tired rag doll in her shoebox bed, with mended seams and sprigs of yarn for hair. How fragile and how durable Emily was.

Then I carefully placed the Sonja Henie doll in her own box and fitted the cover to it. It would be a while before I was ready for her.

CHAPTER VIII

When I was eleven, my talents lay in being able to climb to the top of any tree and to hang from a limb by my knees until my face turned blue. I also had an uncanny knowledge of gardening.

Time had done little to improve my plain appearance, but the defects were somewhat softened by Mother's efforts. A lemon rinse in my hair, more stylish frames for my glasses, and carefully chosen clothes which disguised my now-protruding stomach. I cared more about life than looks, however, and endured Mother's attentions with some exasperation.

Carolyn, at age ten, maintained the quiet composure of her early years. There was a Madonna-like quality about her face, with her large brown eyes, high cheek bones and meditative expression. She moved through life in a detached sort of way, keeping most of her thoughts to herself. During the winter she suffered from chronic bronchitis, and because of this, spent most of her time indoors. Mother gave her light chores to do, and I often heard her say to Betty, "You help Carolyn because she isn't very strong."

Betty was almost thirteen and very grown up. There

was an ethereal beauty in her face and a grace to her mannerisms that suggested the woman she would become. She and Mother shared a love of literature, language, and learning. Each day after school Mother wanted to hear about her Latin assignment, and they sometimes spent hours on an essay. Betty also enjoyed cooking, and made pastries from complicated recipes.

At four years of age, Marilynn was unaware that we were not her real sisters, and I had trouble remembering when I had not thought of her as mine. It had become apparent she and I had similar personalities; the same dauntless reliability on our instincts, open defiance, and the challenge of a dare. If we were not in view of the rest of the family, somebody would be sent to find out what we were doing. Left to our own, Marilynn and I were likely to wander to the other side of the woods to see if the bull that roamed a large fenced-in area really hated the color red. Sometimes we sampled the cans of dog food Daddy stored in the garage. Being older, I took the punishment for our mischief.

Three years with the Nye's had largely dissolved my anxieties, so it was with new-found confidence that I viewed my father's marriage with a mixture of detachment and trepidation. His existence was becoming more shadowy to me. But there was also a fear that threatened my happiness, that someday he might want to take us away.

Mother had taken the telephone call calmly, and afterwards gathered my sisters and me in her room. "Your father has been living in New York, girls," she said. "He has married again and would like you to meet his wife." She said this trying to make her voice sound lively.

"Do you think he will take us away?" Betty asked.

140

"I don't know—we'll have to wait and see," Mother replied.

The morning he was to arrive, Mother shampooed our hair and told us to put on our prettiest dresses. I knew she was nervous by the way she would start to do something and, without finishing, go on to something else. She sang a bit, then her voice trailed off and she gazed out the window. I had seen her this way only once before, and that was when Carolyn had whooping cough and almost died. Mother had sat by the bed night after night as Carolyn struggled for breath, and Mother's strength had seemed to disappear in her concern. Now she had that same drawn look on her face.

It was March, not yet spring, and the air was still and frosty as I walked out to the car with my sisters to greet our father. He was heavier, his silvered gray hair was still thick and wavy, and there were lines around the blue eyes. But yes, I thought, this is my father. This is the man who ran with me in the park, who held my hand and sang "Annie Laurie." This is also the man who turned and walked away from me five years ago at the Catholic Home. It was on that day, I suddenly realized, that I had clenched my fists for the first time.

"Didn't I tell you I had three lovely daughters?" my father asked the lady who had gotten out of the car and was standing beside him.

"Well, well," was all she said as she looked us over.

Mother came to the door, graciously invited my father and his wife to come inside. After she had served them coffee, she excused herself. We were left alone with my father and his new wife, and I was uncomfortable.

I could see my father was happy as he smiled and held his wife's hand. For the first time I looked closely at her. The blue silky dress was fastened at the neck with a gold pendant, and her perfume scented the air. Long dangly earrings and bright red fingernails caught my eye as she clapped her hands together when my father asked, "Shall we take them back with us to New York?"

"Oh, honey, whatever would I do with three little girls?" she laughed. My father joined in her merriment at this outrageous suggestion.

Betty sat quietly, her hands folded in her lap and her face expressing disapproval. Carolyn shared the big armchair with me, and I could tell from the way she kept shifting about that she would be relieved when the visit was over.

It had been five years since my mother died. Whatever knowledge my father may have had of our whereabouts since that day he had never shared with us. As he sat holding the strange lady's hand, I felt a wave of almost anger at his disinterest.

They left rather quickly, saying they had a train to catch. There were awkward hugs and kisses and promises to write. I watched them get in the car together and heard their laughter as they drove away.

My sisters and I walked silently into the house. There was a mutual feeling of disappointment and relief. We knew now our abandonment was complete.

"Did you have a nice visit, girls?" Mother asked, as we helped her prepare supper.

Shrugging her shoulders, Betty replied, "Oh, it was all right."

"I don't like my father or his wife," I said.

"Anne, you must never let me hear you say that again," Mother said. I realized that she was furious.

"I can't help it," I said.

"Don't say 'I can't'—of course you can help it. He is still

142

your father, and you must love and respect him for that if for no other reason."

I was startled at this outburst from her, but it did not really bother me. I had to voice my feelings, and I needed to hear Mother say I was wrong.

At times when I was agitated, I would often find Mother and talk. Without ever stopping what she was doing to sit me down for a lecture, she might say, "Well, Anne, let's look at the whole picture." She was skillful at mixing reprimands with conversation, and would talk in a slow, thought-out way. I sometimes got so interested in what she was saying I would forget my anxieties. Maybe this was part of her method, too.

Now, looking at the expression on Mother's face, I knew my memory of my father would not be of the man I had just seen with his new wife.

Being in the kitchen with Mother and my sisters while we prepared the evening meal had become my favorite time of day. My sisters and I peeled potatoes, made the salad, and set the table while Mother did the cooking. She liked to hear us tell about a movie we had seen or a happening at school. Then she would peek in the oven at her biscuits and say, "Go tell Daddy supper is ready."

But as we silently prepared supper that evening, after seeing my father and his wife, Mother said nothing and did not intrude on the three of us, thinking our separate thoughts.

Later as I puzzled over my father and his new wife, I realized I could not remember her face. Only her high-pitched, incredulous laughter, her trappings and perfume would linger in my mind over the years.

———

It was June of that same year, when I was eleven, that Lynda was born. Mother had told us there was going to be a new baby in the house, but I was not prepared for my feelings for this tiny person.

Recalling the day that Daddy brought Mother and Lynda home from the hospital is easy, because it was one of those special moments that I stored away, to reflect on later. Daddy was all proud smiles as he opened the door on Mother's side of the car. My sisters and I had gathered close by, with Marilynn in front of us. Mother beamed as she looked at us and asked, "How are my girls?"

Then Daddy took the small bundle from her lap and handed it to me. "Here's your new baby sister," he said.

I, the awkward and willful girl—the perpetual scabs on my knees were evidence of my clumsiness, and seldom a day passed that I was not punished for some act of obstinance. Daddy had chosen me to be the first to hold the new baby.

I walked slowly into the house, sat carefully in the rocking chair by the fireplace, and folded back the pink blanket for a look at my baby sister. Her large violet eyes stared back at me, and I knew an absolute joy in holding this new life that had come into my own.

Daddy went into the Army in 1942—soon after Lynda was a year old—and Mother resumed teaching to help out financially. Although we had occasional household help, Mother was never idle, with her school responsibilities and raising five girls.

Betty, a tall, willowy fourteen-year-old, was very much in charge of her life. Carolyn was eleven, a good student and a perfectionist in her chores. Marilynn had started first grade that fall, and it fell upon Betty to see that she got to and from school safely. This turned out not to be easy. Marilynn refused to be helped on or off the bus, and

144

her legs weren't long enough to reach the steps. She repeatedly lost her lunch, and one day she swallowed a small bolt from a seat in the auditorium and had to be rushed to the hospital. Although I admired Marilynn's spunk, I did not interfere with Betty's discipline of her.

Lynda was like a doll to us. We enjoyed dressing her and argued over who would take her for a walk in her stroller. I went to sleep at night hearing Mother sing "Swing Low, Sweet Chariot" as she rocked Lynda to sleep. It was always soothing to hear her there in the quiet darkness. The news of the Second World War had a frightening effect on me—and on most children. Dreadful battles were shown in the Paramount newsreels, and H.V. Kaltenborn's evening news was always grim. My sisters and I were sure that bombs would soon hit Charlotte, especially when there were blackouts and air-raid drills. But all this was forgotten as I listened at night to Mother and the rhythmic creak of her rocker.

I had only twice thought Mother was unfair to me. She was the kind of person who looked at life objectively and with compassion. But she never thought of herself as being so virtuous, and she would smile now at my remembrance of these injustices.

She had grown up in the Great Smokey Mountains of North Carolina, the daughter of a stern intellectual man who said little and demanded much of his children. Her mother was an outspoken, good-natured, and hardworking woman. Mother inherited some of the qualities of both her parents.

Her sense of properness came from her father. To be dressed correctly told him a great deal about a person, and he passed this on to his children. For Mother, who was slightly overweight, her fetish was her corset. On one occasion she was getting ready to go to her teachers' meetings when she could not find her corset. She was never seen in public without this piece of apparel, which my sisters and I often joked about. She accused me of hiding the corset—because I could be guilty of such mischief—and sent me to my room while a frantic search was made for the garment. She found it on the clothesline where she herself had left it. Then she went off to her meeting, leaving me in my room. She never apologized for this accusation.

The other injustice occurred when I was twelve years old. While Daddy was in the Army, my sisters and I had to learn to do many things to help out in his absence. We had always raised chickens—some for the eggs and some for eating. One afternoon Mother sent me into the chicken yard to pick out a "Rhode Island Red that would be just right for frying." When I had located one, she got out the small axe, handed it to me, and said, "Now cut off its head."

"I can't!" I screamed.

"Don't say that, Anne, and calm down," she said.

I took the chicken by the feet as she instructed, laid its head across a board, closed my eyes, and raised and lowered the axe six times before I came down on the chicken's neck. When I opened my eyes, I saw to my horror the chicken had gotten up and walked away with its head dangling to the side. My knees grew weak and my vision blurred, but Mother gave me a push and said, "Go get that chicken and finish your job."

When I had finished beheading the poor thing, Mother got out a pail of scalding water, doused the chicken in it, and plucked the feathers, making sure I learned each step of the process. Then she held up the denuded bird and said, "Come with me and I will show you how to cut it up for frying." The sight of the chicken without a head and the smell of the hot feathers had reached the bottom of my stomach. To dismember it now was out of the question. I fled to the back of the garage where I was sick.

———————

Sitting with Mother on a summer afternoon on the porch—while she drank iced tea and picked dead leaves off geraniums in a pot near her—I sensed the seriousness of her mood. I was almost fourteen, and I very much liked these times when just the two of us sat and talked. She had a way of putting everything in its proper place.

She seemed somber as she said, without looking at me, "You are going into high school this fall, Anne, and we are going to have to do something about your grades." I looked away and did not answer. My attitude toward school distressed her, and I knew our time together on this day might not be a happy one.

Without any overtures, she went on, "I have decided to send you away to school." I turned and looked at her in disbelief. I wanted to say "I can't—it's unfair!" But I knew there was no need to say either.

Betty, who was a year ahead of me in school, had been at the top of her class in every grade. At first I tried to be just like her, but I could not. I would watch as she read, and wonder how she could find so much pleasure in it. She loved her geography books, her Latin books, and her math books. She was the champion speller in the school, the most beautiful girl, and probably the kindest person I will ever know. She was not one to judge people by their intelligence or lack of it; I was her sister, and she loved me for that. Whatever else I was or was not did not matter to her.

The teachers, however, had a different point of view, and for all my school years I had been plagued by, "Why can't you be like Betty?" After my first year I gave up the struggle. Life was to be lived—not burdened by study of the terrain of Egypt, a mathematical equation, or a foreign language I would never use. I was reproached by my teachers for being stupid. At the end of each grading period, Mother would look at my report card, shake her head sadly and say, "Anne, you must stop your woolgathering and get on with your studies." I pretended that none of it mattered.

Watching my struggles and knowing me better than anyone else did, Mother had made this decision. I knew that I must trust her, as I had since my sisters and I came to live with her more than six years earlier.

With no enthusiasm I looked at the school brochures. We settled on Crossnore boarding school, located in the Blue Ridge Mountains of North Carolina. The pamphlet we had received showed only one picture of the school and said it was founded by Dr. and Mrs. Eustace Sloop "for the purpose of educating underprivileged children." I was attracted to the line that said, "No formal dress for students is required." Mother liked the part that said, "Each student has a job on the campus."

On a morning early in September I said goodbye to my sisters, and Mother and I drove off to the Blue Ridge Mountains—Mother with hopes I would become an honor student, I feeling unhappiness, rejection, and fear.

The air smelled of the newness of autumn. Goldenrod bloomed along the sides of the road, farmers were cutting corn, and pumpkins were almost ripe. Passing through towns, the signs in the shop windows said, "Back to School Supplies." It was not a time of year I looked forward to.

At the foot of the mountains Mother and I stopped for a

picnic lunch she had prepared. Looking ahead as far as I could see were mountains. A soft blue haze formed across the tops, obstructing their shapes and heights. It was beautiful but forbidding, and I wondered where in that blue mist was Crossnore, and what it would be like.

Mother loved the mountains, and to her the sight of these great hills looming before us was exciting. "Aren't they magnificent? You are going to love it there," she said, elated. How could she be so happy when I felt so sad? I wondered.

After lunch we continued our drive into the high blue haze, then down again and back up to greater heights. I knew Mother was right: they were breathtaking. It was like entering a land where no one had been before. Here and there leaves were beginning to take on their fall colors. The dark lustrous foliage of mountain laurel glistened in the sunlight. The floor of the forest was covered with wild ferns. Woodchucks, chipmunks, and squirrels played along the roadsides. Once a deer ran in front of us. Water, clear and cold, trickled down rocks that jutted out from the mountainside. The dark shadows of the forest closed around us. Then the sun flashed through the trees, like sapphires lighting our way. There were signs saying, "Falling Rock" and "Do Not Litter" which seemed alien in this beautiful place.

When we reached the top of the mountain, Mother and I got out of the car and looked out over the valley. The blue haze was now below us. It had swallowed the serpentine roads we had just passed over. My ears popped from the altitude and my stomach still churned from the twisty turns, but I found myself caught up in Mother's excitement. We walked a little way down the mountain as she pointed out wildflowers. Her face was flushed. "Oh, look, ladyslippers, trillium, smell the wild ginger!" I knew if she had her spade, she would have dug up half the mountainside and taken it home with her.

Returning to the car, we drove further into the mountains, then came upon a small village. A gas station, one or two stores, a church, and a few houses. A boy walked along with a dog, a lady in a bonnet was bringing in her laundry, and a young man tinkered with his car. Other families sat on their porches, rocking peacefully in the autumn afternoon. Mother—usually quite shy—waved as we drove by, and they waved back to her.

Our trip continued through other small villages and an insulated world of nature. We stopped at one little town while Mother looked at handmade quilts and bought pickle relish in a country store.

It was late afternoon when we saw the sign that said "Crossnore." At first it seemed like all the other villages—a store, a cafe, a movie theater. High up a hill was a small white wooden church. We saw another sign, for Crossnore school, and turned up a gravel road. We passed a frame building with "Sale Room" painted across the front, then two small stone buildings—one marked "Weaving Room," the other "Sewing." Mother, who had a special affection for mountain crafts, said, "Now won't that be nice, Anne— you will learn to weave and sew." This appealed to me and I began to be more interested in the place. Finding a sign that read "Registration," we came to a low white building where students were milling about. The brochure had said the school took students from grades one through twelve, so I was not surprised to see children of all ages.

Waiting in line to register, I noticed the lady at the desk. Her hair was a cloud of white, and the lines in her face deepened in the most beautiful way as she greeted each child with a smile. Her dark blue dress with its lace collar hung loosely on her stout body, and her glasses kept slipping down her nose. Without getting up, she rolled her chair back to a window, called to some boys to unload some boxes for her, then greeted more students with, "I'm so glad to see you again." Everything about her indicated she was in charge, and she clearly loved what she was doing.

Stepping up to the desk, my mother said, "I am Mrs. Nye and this is my daughter Anne." The woman got up, clasped her hands together in a spontaneous gesture of joy, and said, "Anne, I am Mrs. Sloop, and I am happy you are going to be with us." I was so enchanted by her that I could not, at that moment, say a word.

"Anne is going into the ninth grade this year, and I would like to have monthly reports on her work," Mother said.

"Never fear, I keep tabs on all my children. If she does not do well, you will know about it," replied Mrs. Sloop. There was a firmness in her voice now, but she smiled, took my hand in both of hers and said, "You are going to be all right here." Her hands were soft and marked with the brown spots of age, but touching them I sensed the strength and understanding of this woman.

A tenth-grade student had been assigned to take us to the dormitory, and along the way he pointed out the names of the several dormitories, the dining room, the infirmary, the music building, and the gymnasium. The beauty of the mountains was here—there were no sidewalks or asphalt streets, only paths and dirt roads worn smooth by constant use. There were streams with little wooden bridges, wildflowers were left to grow wherever their seeds had fallen, and if a tree stood in the way of a path, the path simply went around it.

The big girls dormitory where I was to stay was built largely of rock gathered from the mountainsides. The walls in the lounge were paneled oak and obviously decorated by the girls themselves. There was a picture of Frank Sinatra on one wall, Van Johnson and June Allyson were on another. There was a large fireplace with some rocking chairs in front of it. The only other furniture was a piano and four long tables with benches around them. The room smelled as if it had been closed during the hot summer months and was now open to let the fresh air of fall come in.

Girls were running about everywhere in a state of happy confusion. One looked for an ironing board, another emerged from the shower in a robe. There were squeals of laughter coming from the rooms as we walked down the hall on the second floor to my room.

Sitting on the strange bed that was to be mine, Mother put her hand on my arm and said, "Anne, this is your chance to do your best. Don't let yourself down." She was not a demonstrative person, and never one for impulsive hugs and kisses.

"Now don't lose your money, and be sure to write," she said without looking at me. Then her voice choked ever so slightly. "Be sure to wear your scarf when the weather gets cold." Getting up and walking toward the door, she looked around the room as if to satisfy herself that it would be all right for me. I realized this was as painful for her as it was for me, but I could not let her know it. Not now, when I had come this far without breaking down. I wanted to show her this did not matter to me. Her eyes were tearing but she did not cry as she said, "Goodbye, Anne. We will look forward to seeing you at Thanksgiving."

After she had left, I walked to the landing of the stairs and looked out the window. I saw her get in her car and drive away. Nothing in my life had prepared me for the loneliness I felt at that moment. It was the first time I had been separated from my sisters, and already I ached with longing for them. My eyes burned, my throat began to close—finally I put my face in my hands and cried.

"Hey kiddo, isn't your name Anne?" asked a voice behind me. Without turning I said, "Yes." Wheeling me around and looking straight into my teary eyes, she said, "I'm your roommate. My name is Dottie. Well, actually it is Dorothy, but nobody calls me that."

Dottie, I found, was a grade below me, but we were close to the same age. She had brown eyes, deep dimples in her cheeks, and curly hair. She was lively, full of wit, and not about to let anyone around her have a serious moment. She linked her arm through mine and we went to our room together.

And so the next six years of my life began on a September afternoon, in the village of Crossnore, in the Blue Ridge Mountains, with a girl named Dottie.

CHAPTER IX

No one knew better than I how quickly and cruelly the patterns of life can be rearranged. But knowing this did not make my first weeks at Crossnore any less painful.

Once again I felt abandoned, this time by Mother. I had allowed myself to love her, always knowing there can be no permanency to a foster child's life. I had even come to believe that she was my real mother, and that what had happened before her did not really happen at all. But I realized that this love had disarmed me. What would sustain me in these new feelings of anger and rejection?

The mountains rising above the school seemed to close around and suffocate me as I thought of that great stretch of miles between my sisters and me. I remembered the times they had stood beside me with the brown cardboard suitcases. The anguish of the years after my mother's death swept over me, renewed and intensified. I thought too about my father, groping for some sense of attachment to him—but there was none.

Then I realized Dottie had been talking to me. "Are you going to stand by that window and mope all evening?" she asked.

She was busy hanging her clothes in her side of the closet. She had been cheerful all afternoon, and during dinner her infectious laughter had allowed me briefly to forget my loneliness.

"What else is there to do?" I asked.

"There's going to be a square dance downstairs in the lounge in a few minutes. You'd better be getting ready," she replied.

When I asked if she was going to the dance, she said, "You bet I am!"

"I don't think I will," I said.

"Come on, don't be an old stick-in-the-mud. Get your hair combed and let's go."

"But I don't know how to square dance."

"Neither do I, but I'm sure gonna learn."

Then she went through my closet to see if I had a sweater she could wear with her gray skirt. The next thing I knew I was in the lounge, wearing a green blouse that belonged to Dottie, and she was standing beside me in my blue sweater.

Frosty evenings come early to the mountains, and the big fire in the stone fireplace crackled and popped while the musicians tuned their fiddles and banjoes. The housemothers were greeting the boys at the door, and the room felt warm and friendly.

A nice-looking boy with dark, curly hair came over to me. "Hi, my name is Roger," he said. "What's yours?"

I remember still my adolescent blush, the stumbling for words, and the sheer joy that comes to every fourteen-year-old girl when that first boy asks her to dance.

The music started, the caller said, "Grab your partner and promenade left," and the sound of fiddles, clapping and stomping echoed across the mountains.

The dances were called by Obie Johnson. Mr. Obie, as

we called him, was a tall, wiry man in his forties, with a lopsided grin and a talent for mountain music and dance. During the intermission he sang a few ballads. One favorite went something like this:

> "Great grandad, when he was young,
> Barred his door with a wagon tongue,
> Great granddad was a busy man,
> He cooked his grub in a frying pan.
> He picked his teeth with a hunting knife,
> And wore the same suit all his life."

Later that night I again stood by the window in the room I shared with Dottie and tried to sort out my feelings. My aloneness had seemed to dissipate in the warmth of the evening. What was there about this place that would not let me indulge in pity? What had Mother meant when she had said, "It is here you will find yourself, Anne?"

———————

The first month I struggled through my classes, daydreaming about home and my sisters. Mrs. Carpenter kept me after school to go over an algebra assignment. Mr. Woodside called me to the board to work a physics problem for which I was not prepared. No one ever tried to hornswoggle Mr. Woodside. You simply stood there while his piercing brown eyes stripped your mind bare and your brain refused to function. If you did the problem wrong, he erased it and watched quietly as you struggled with a different approach.

Homework after school was done on the long tables in the dormitory lounge. The housemothers sat in their rocking chairs by the fire and occasionally looked up from their reading or sewing to admonish a girl for talking or giggling.

True to her word, Mrs. Sloop did keep track of the children. I had spent my study time writing endless letters home, but this indifference to school came to a halt with my first report card. I was summoned to her office before my grades had a chance to reach Mother in Charlotte.

To be called to Mrs. Sloop's office for misbehavior or bad grades was a tremulous experience. Leaning forward, resting her arms on her desk, she got your full attention by gazing straight into your eyes without blinking. Her speech became a bit louder and more insistent, punctuated by a sudden pounding on the desk with her hand. Then she told stories of ne'er-do wells and said what a terrible thing it was to waste one's mind. But she knew the goodness in every child, and before the lecture ended, her voice would soften and she would smile. "I hear you are handling your job on the campus in a very responsible way. Now let's see if you can't do as well with your studies."

I sat rigid in front of her desk, trying not to look at her. But when our eyes met I was so mesmerized that there was no turning away.

"Are you disappointed in yourself?" she asked quietly.

"Yes," I replied.

"That is what matters the most, Anne," she said.

Then she picked up the telephone and called my mother in Charlotte. "Mrs. Nye, I have your daughter here and I want you both to hear this." She was talking so loudly that I was sure she had deafened my mother. "The tests given the students show Anne is one of the brightest in her class, but she is barely passing her subjects." She shouted into the telephone, all the while looking straight at me. "But Anne's next grades are going to be a big improvement." After a few pleasantries, she hung up the telephone and walked to the window to look out at the darkening sky.

My shame made me wish I could just disappear and not have to face her when she turned around. Quietly she said, "Come here, Anne." Standing beside her, looking out the window, I saw a boy making his way across the campus in a wheelchair. Neither of us spoke until the boy was no longer in sight. Turning to me, cupping my chin in her hand, she said, "You have so much, my dear, don't throw it away." I quickly said goodnight. As I walked to the dormitory I smiled, thinking she had not once compared me to my sister.

My first job on campus was as waitress in the big dining room. Dottie was also a waitress, and from the first day she tackled her work with deftness and humor. She was aware of the smaller children in a way that did not fit in with her happy-go-lucky personality. I sometimes heard her say to a little one, "Drink all your milk" or, "Put your coat on before you go outside." And she wasn't above sneaking an extra dessert for a child who had caught her sympathy.

Mrs. Bell—Ma Bell as she was known to us—was in charge of the dining room. An immaculately groomed lady, she ran her dining room like a fine restaurant: silver had to be placed just so, always serve from the left, and our aprons had to be spotless. She sometimes scolded us for riding up and down in the dumb-waiter when we should be working, but she called us her "children" and treated us with affection.

Our jobs changed every month, and it was my second assignment, as monitor in the little boys dormitory, that gave me the greatest satisfaction—so much so that I requested that job for the remainder of the year.

Forty little boys lived there, ranging in age from six to ten. Each morning I went to their dormitory after breakfast, saw that they made their beds and were prepared for school. I was also reponsible for their after-school activities, and I assisted the housemother in helping them with homework in the evening.

This seemed a formidable task that first morning as I approached the long frame building that was their dormitory. The housemother, a plump lady with red hair and a deep throaty laugh, introduced me to the boys, gave me a wink, and disappeared into her apartment. They were all mine, she seemed to be saying.

I remember thinking how small the children were, and yet how old they seemed. Their tousled heads and cherubic faces contradicted their self-sufficing manner. I looked at the large squarish room, lined with beds, grey metal lockers against one wall. The October sun slanting through the curtainless windows outlined the shapes of forty little boys standing motionless. For a moment I felt that I was standing with them, that I was one of them. I could feel a scratchy, brown wool coat, and from far off a voice saying, "Come with me, you are leaving here today."

A tug on my arm broke the spell. Looking down I saw a small boy wearing worn mittens, his shoes tied in ridiculous knots.

"I'm all ready for school," he said.

Remembering where I was, I knelt down and tied his shoes properly. "Thank you, ma'am," he said.

I looked at him, and suddenly my sense of self turned outward. We are in this together, I thought.

It is strange as I think about it now, but none of the children at Crossnore School discussed with other children why they were there. Sometimes one might mention a parent, another might talk about an aunt or a sister, but these conversations never went far. There was no separation at Crossnore of rich and poor, or smart and dull either. Children from broken or impoverished homes and from orphanages in the Carolinas and other states attended the school. There were also a few students here because their parents liked the school, its discipline and sense of duty.

At first I saw in the little boys a resignation to their life here. Then I began to feel their acceptance—their letting go of the past. This is not to say it was easy for all of them. They were children, and many times there were tears for no apparent reason. And I came to recognize that a stalwart attitude was often a disguise for fear.

There was eight-year-old Sammy—big for his age and the only loner in the group. He kept with him at all times a brown paper bag that had been twisted and untwisted at the top so many times it had begun to crumble.

Sammy was often missing from the group, and I would have to go looking for him. One afternoon I found him sitting on the coal pile behind the dormitory. He was smoking. He inhaled, squinted his eyes, and blew the smoke out, just like a grown man.

"Aren't you afraid you'll catch the place on fire?" I asked.

"Hell, no," he responded, almost with disdain.

For a moment I was a bit frightened of him, but I stood shivering in the cold until he finished his cigarette, then took him back to the dormitory.

The next time I found him smoking, I asked him to stop.

"Cain't," he said.

"Don't say you can't, of course you can," I told him.

He looked away, and kept right on puffing.

Somehow I could not report him to the housemother. But I wanted very much to make him stop smoking, and also to find why he treasured that bag.

I liked Sammy. His eyes were as black as his hair, his

pants too short, his feet too big. And he could do long division in his head.

Discovering what was in the bag happened late one afternoon when I had to take him to the infirmary for a head cold. He had a fever, and the nurse insisted that he stay overnight. Before I left him there, he asked that I go to his locker and bring him the bag.

I felt guilty prying into Sammy's private world but I had to know what was in the bag. When I returned to the infirmary, I stopped on the lighted porch long enough to look inside the bag. There were a half-dozen cigarette butts (not surprising), a police whistle, and a picture. I looked at the picture closely. It had been cut in half, and was bent and ragged around the edges. The black-and-white print was of a woman and a small boy sitting on a fence rail. The boy I recognized as Sammy, somewhat younger. The lady must be his mother, I guessed.

As I closed the bag and twisted it shut, I thought about walnuts, candy, and a shriveled red balloon in a brown cardboard suitcase. I knew what this bag meant to Sammy. I went on to his room, hoping the nurse would not follow.

"Please don't smoke in here, Sammy," I whispered, handing him the bag.

"You looked," he said, turning away from me.

"Yes," I replied.

Neither of us said anything for a moment. Then I asked, "Is the lady in the picture your mother?"

"She was my mother, but not anymore."

"Why not?"

"Cause she's gone up north, and she ain't never coming back."

"How do you know that?"

"That's what my daddy did a long time ago, and he never came back."

"Was it your daddy you cut out of the picture?"

"Yeah. Now shut up and stay out of my business."

He was right—it was none of my business. I changed the subject. "You know we could use that whistle you have."

"What for?" he asked.

"Well, when we all go for a hike, I have to do a lot of yelling to get the boys to stay together. I thought you could help me by using your whistle."

"Maybe," he said.

I watched him go to sleep. Before I left I hid the brown bag in his shoe, so the nurse couldn't find it.

Sammy did use his whistle, a little reluctantly at first. But when he found that the children responded, it made him feel important.

Throughout October, with the mountains in gaudy dress of yellow, red, and orange, the boys and I went for long hikes, Sammy by my side with his whistle. Sometimes we sang silly songs or played hide and seek along the way. We talked of many things, how rocks are formed, how to tell the age of a tree, what we would do if a bear appeared. But we did not talk of home. I knew that the lives of these boys had not been that much different from mine. And like my little friends and charges, I too was letting go of the past.

Mrs. Sloop often came to the dormitory to visit the boys. I can see her standing in the middle of the room, a tumble of small boys around her. Even in the coldest weather she wore her little hat with flowers on it. Fatigue might show behind her big smile, but when one of the boys told her about a home run in baseball or a school achievement, she hugged him and told him how wonderful he was.

The first time Mrs. Sloop visited, I saw Sammy stand outside the group. How carefully he worked at concealing his emotions, his expressionless black eyes giving no clue to his thoughts. Mrs. Sloop ignored him until she was ready to leave. "Sammy, your housemother has some folders she wants me to take to my office," she said. "Would you come along with me and carry them?"

I watched them slowly descend the hill together, Sammy keeping pace with Mrs. Sloop's deliberate steps. Then I saw her arm go around his shoulder, and I knew that this insightful woman would manage somehow to lessen his burden.

Fall ended and the mountains disappeared in snow. My boys and I trudged to the top of Christmas Tree Hill. Why it was called this I never knew, since there wasn't a tree on it. It was just a high knoll, perfect for sledding. No one had a sled, of course, so we sat in a long line with our legs locked around the person ahead, and holding on to their shoulders, down the hill we went. At the bottom we'd end up in a pile, then lie there feeling the snowflakes melt on our cheeks. At times like this I lost all track of distance and memory.

———————

The village of Crossnore was two hours from Asheville by bus, a bit less if you went by car. The story goes that somewhere around 1850 George Crossnore had a small store here in the Blue Ridge. The mailman making his trip through the mountains always stopped to talk with George. Then one of the women up in the hills, tired of traveling twelve miles to a post office for her mail, suggested that a post office be put in George's store. The mailman induced the government to set one up there and to give the place the name of Crossnore. George left the village some fifty years later. Apparently no one knew where he had come from or where he went when he left.

When I arrived in Crossnore in 1944, the town had four buildings and two churches. At the center of town was a circle formed by a low rock wall; in the middle of the circle was a drinking fountain. This was the meeting place for the townspeople. Sometimes men returning from work in the evenings parked their cars, ambled over to the circle, sat on the rock wall, and talked. The Aldridge boys were usually there, watching for boarding school girls to go by. I liked the Aldridge boys—one of them taught me to square dance.

There was the community store, offering everything from food to farm tools. Dottie and I went there often to buy school supplies, lingering to look at some new merchandise or stand by the stove and talk to the townspeople.

During my first year at Crossnore, the theater was an old frame building. The wooden floors squeaked and the hard seats had come unbolted from the floor. Just below the screen was a potbellied stove. Every so often the theater owner would bring in a bucket of coal and stoke the fire. As he poked at the fire, sparks would shoot out, causing people sitting near the stove to get up and move. Then there would be calls from the back of the theater, "Hurry up, we can't see the picture!" The boys also had the girls convinced there were rats and spiders in the place, but it never prevented us from going there.

Later, a new theater was built with a carpeted floor and plush seats, and the old theater was turned into a roller skating rink. There was no charge for skating. Whoever was there tended the fire in the potbellied stove, and the last ones to leave in the evening put the fire out.

The favorite place for the boarding school students was the cafe. Dottie and I went there often, shared a milk shake, and listened to the jukebox. Sometimes, the lady who cooked there would say, "Guess what, girls I just made some apple pies." Then she gave us a piece, pretending she wanted us to test it for doneness, because she knew we could not always afford to pay.

The Greyhound bus made two stops a day at the cafe, and anyone returning from a trip would come in, have a cup of coffee, and talk about where they had been. It was usually Asheville, over Roan Mountain into Tennessee, or maybe north to Roanoke.

The Crossnore post office was next to the cafe, and each resident had a box there, since there was no house-to-house delivery. Mr. Dellinger, the postmaster, called everybody by their first name, and he could tell you almost each piece of mail that had come through his post office for the past twenty years. He was very proud of his "government-paid" job—it gave him a connection with "those people in Washington." He occasionally expounded on the subject of "this administration" or "what will the government do next?" We all respected him.

On a high hill overlooking the village was the little white Baptist church. I remember that you had to climb seventy-two steps to reach it. It was full every Sunday, and on Wednesday nights some of the townspeople held prayer meetings there. Sometimes the church was used as a hall for town meetings.

The Presbyterian church, where I went, was around a bend in the road, up a hill and across a bridge. Standing apart from the village amid tall pine trees and blue spruce, I could feel tranquility from the moment I crossed the bridge and started up the steps. It was built in the 1920s by Will Franklin, the finest carpenter around. Mrs. Sloop, after much pleading with him to build the church, said that if he didn't, the Lord would surely punish him.

Being a God-fearing man, he started on it right away, gathering rocks from the riverbanks and timbers from the nearby forest. He was proud of his finished work—the pulpit with its metal slab made to look like an open book; the two posts for flowers, each encircled with twelve tiny stones to represent the twelve tribes of Israel; and the high vaulted ceilings that gave the interior the appearance of a cathedral.

Dottie and I sang in the choir there on Sunday mornings, and all the children gathered there again on Sunday evenings when Mrs. Sloop would talk to us about everything from current events to social manners. Then we would leave the church to return to the school, holding hands and singing "God be with you till we meet again." I can still hear the voices of the children on those starlit nights as we walked back to our dormitories.

———————

Most of the people in the town had lived there all their lives, as had their families before them. Many were related, either by blood or marriage. Some of the men were skilled craftsmen, some were farmers, others worked in the nearby towns of Spruce Pine, Newland, and Blowing Rock. One rich family owned a mica mine, one the community store, a third the cafe and theater. Crossnore ladies shared their talents, such as weaving and sewing, with the boarding school. Some of the women were school teachers, some worked in the office, the kitchen or laundry. All were dedicated to their families, to God, and to helping others.

Although these people were knowledgeable about world affairs, they never got excited about events or changes. Some of their men had been killed in wars; they suffered the same ills and misfortunes of all humanity, but they bore their adversities in silence and with grace. Every fall they welcomed the boarding school children and gave them love.

I never heard of a murder, rape, or theft in the town. Once or twice some boys took a chicken from somebody's coop. They confessed their prank, and the owner would say, "Now you boys know better than to stir up my chickens in the middle of the night. Go on off about your business and leave my place alone." There were no hard feelings toward the boys, and if the incident were described to someone, it would be with a chuckle and the remembrance that the owner had once done the same thing.

It was said there was a still in somebody's barn. But we all knew this couldn't be true, because Mrs. Sloop had disposed of the last still back in the 1930s, hauling it down the mountainside in her wheelbarrow. The mere mention of the word "moonshine" back then sent her scurrying into the hills to find its source, bring in the sheriff, and dispose of it.

There was an Oxford graduate who lived alone up in the hills. I saw him only once. He had bright red hair and a bushy red beard, and he was always barefoot. He didn't look like a college graduate to me, but they said he was very intelligent and that he liked his solitude. The residents would give him a "Good morning, sir. Fine day, isn't it?" He would reply in an amiable way, without ever starting up a conversation.

The only other person whose life history was not known to the townspeople was a man called "The Hermit." He was small, with a whiskered face and shy manners, and traveled about with his little dog "Happy." He wore an old felt hat and baggy pants held up with wide suspenders.

His needs were supplied by handouts from the village people, and at night he just disappeared. Though he was a curiosity to everyone, he was harmless, and no attempt was made to pry into his life.

George Crossnore had given the town its name, but it was Dr. Eustace Sloop and his wife, Dr. Mary Martin Sloop, who brought health and learning to this part of the Blue Ridge.

They had graduated from medical school at Davidson College in North Carolina in 1915. Instead of going to China or Africa as so many missionaries did in those days, they chose to become medical missionaries in the Appalachian range along the Tennessee-North Carolina border.

They quickly became circuit-riding doctors, traveling through the mountains over treacherous, unpaved roads. They often performed surgery under trees and delivered babies by candlelight in the mountain cabins.

While making doctor rounds one day with her husband, Mrs. Sloop met Hepsy, a bright and lively mountain girl of thirteen. When she learned the child was not in school and that her father wanted to marry her off, Mrs. Sloop took Hepsy home, determined to find a way to educate her.

Pondering over how to finance this, and also how to clothe the girl since she had only the one dress, Mrs. Sloop wrote to some relatives, asking for used clothing. There had been a recent death in the family, and the relatives sent off a trunk load of used mourning clothes. Discouraged at the sight of all those black dresses, Mrs. Sloop was hanging them out to air when one of the neighbor women came by. She thought the black dresses beautiful, and asked to buy one. She went off, told others about them, and soon all the dresses were sold. From that first sale of used clothing, Hepsy was educated, and the selling of used clothing and other articles is still a source of income for the school. From all over the country a great variety of used and discarded items are shipped to Crossnore. The Sale Room lures people from all the little mountain towns around.

Dottie and I liked to go there and try on the fancy hats, high-heeled shoes, and taffeta ball gowns. They sometimes smelled of expensive perfumes, and I would imagine an elegant lady going to a party dressed in this finery. Almost every era of time was represented in that room, from highbutton shoes to modern sandals, dresses with bustles, blue jeans, cameo brooches, gaudy earrings.

Building her own school during the 1920s and '30s was a difficult task for Mrs. Sloop. Her first school, a one-room lean-to, was soon overflowing, with students sleeping overnight at the school since there were no roads and they came from long distances. Some of the mountain folk were opposed to all this education and attempted to keep their children away from school. But their attitude changed when they learned that Mrs. Sloop would take them to court and they could be sent to jail.

Mrs. Sloop made her requests—which were more like demands—to state and local government officials for roads in the mountains and for a better school at Crossnore. In time she got all of this. Roads were put through, some eventually paved. A dormitory was built by the children who that first year had slept in the frame lean-to. Later more dormitories and classroom buildings went up, and Crossnore school continues today much as it had in those early beginnings.

Mrs. Sloop had the courage to stand before awesome philanthropic groups asking their support for her school, but she also had the sensitivity to see into the heart of a first-grader who had been abandoned by his parents. From the day that she found a way to educate Hepsy until her death in 1962, she spent her life ministering to children. No one was too poor or too ignorant to go to her school. If students came to her as failures, she had a way of showing those children their desirable qualities. She was staunch in her belief that each child be given a chance.

Mrs. Sloop's husband—the "Doctor" as he was called by everyone—took great pride in his wife's work, although his own life was dedicated to medicine. Through his efforts a hospital was built, staffed by himself, their daughter Emma, also a physician, and their son Bill, who was a dentist.

Dr. Eustace Sloop, a dry-witted man, was well over six feet tall, with massive shoulders, white hair and a full white beard. He had the countenance of a man pleased with his accomplishments and fully content in his work.

There were many stories about the Doctor and how he managed to rid the mountain people of their mythical cures for illness, but my favorite is how he brought electricity to the area in the 1920s.

Wanting to improve conditions at the school, Mrs. Sloop had written to her brother who taught at Davidson College, to ask if they could have an old generator that was stored in the College basement. Then Dr. Sloop ordered the necessary electrical parts from his Sears, Roebuck catalogue. As he traveled through the mountains on horseback visiting his patients, he read manuals on electricity and wiring. The generator arrived, the parts arrived, and with the help of a neighbor, everything was installed and connected. The bulb was placed in the socket and when the switch was turned on, the Doctor had his electric light. Word spread quickly about this wonder, and everybody wanted electric lights. The answer was to build a dam and a power plant, and few years later Dr. Sloop saw to it that this was constructed.

Every Tuesday the Doctor and Mrs. Sloop went into Asheville, he to get supplies for his hospital, she to speak to a group or go over school finances with her banker. The order of their Tuesdays never changed for as long as I knew them. They went their separate ways, then met at the S. & W. cafeteria for dinner and afterwards to a movie. After I began working in Mrs. Sloop's office, I went with them many times on these Tuesday trips. Dr. Sloop might choose to sleep through the movie, but he never departed from his schedule.

To walk down the street beside him was like being a celebrity. Without knowing who he was, all eyes would be on him, doors were opened for him, people stepped aside to let him pass. By his bearing you knew he was someone great—could he be a man of nobility or even a character from some legend? Whoever he was, when he smiled at you, it was like being touched by a saint.

From the moment I met Dottie I took pleasure in her. It may have been the natural way that she took life in stride. It may have been that she gave me the confidence I needed that first day. The certainty that she would always be my friend had come in some fine way from the very beginning. The essence of our friendship was its entireness. I cannot remember those six years at Crossnore without Dottie being a part of it. The walks over fallen leaves, the toboggan slides down the slopes, swimming at the dam, consoling each other over a poor grade or a lost boyfriend—these things I remember and so much more about her.

Dottie received letters and a monthly allowance from a woman in Asheville, but she never talked about it and I gave it no thought. I did ask once if she had brothers or sisters. She said she had a brother who had died in infancy.

She went home with me to Charlotte during a holiday, and then one weekend, invited me to go home with her. Her "home," it turned out, was an orphanage in Asheville, filled with little children who ran to greet her at the door. At first I was stunned, but when I saw Dottie cuddling a small child while another pulled at her skirt, I understood why I felt so close to this girl. I asked why she had not told me about the orphanage. She shrugged, "Everybody has a little sack of rocks to carry—I guess this is mine."

It might be said that Dottie and I supported each other in our friendship. But I think it is better said that we had found in ourselves the strength for our own survival.

Sammy grew into a tall and confident teenager, moving into the big boys dormitory two years after I first knew him. He had been right when he said that he would not hear from his mother again. Perhaps he still has that ragged photograph, but I am certain that his anger is gone. He will hold no grievance against her or his father, both of whom had, in succession, abandoned him.

Crossnore is known as a school for underprivileged children, but most there would consider themselves fortunate. They have learned early that life can be unfair and have made their adjustments to it. And the love they have been denied elsewhere they will find at Crossnore.

"In the little world in which children exist," said Charles Dickens, "there is nothing so finely perceived and so finely felt as injustice."

To the orphan and foster child, life can be a series of injustices, each more overwhelming than the last. The first and most ready response is anger and rebellion, and

172

that response can continue after the reason for it is gone. So it might have been with me, had I not had the quieting experience of Crossnore. There I ceased striking out, and dropped my rebellious defense against a world I had not trusted or understood.

I went home to Charlotte for my summers and holidays, but I was always eager to return to Crossnore. I was at peace with myself here among the mountain people, with their simple expectations, gentle manners, unhurried pace, and joy in living. The six years went quickly, and the mountains that once seemed to suffocate me now rose like a giant fortress around the school, protecting us from the outside world.

CHAPTER X

〰〰〰〰〰〰〰〰〰〰〰

Leaving the mountains and the mountain people after six years among them was a painful day in my life.

At graduation I had received my two-year certificate in business administration, the Danforth Foundation award, the Crossnore merit award, and of all things, a certificate for perfect attendance. Now I walked alone one last time over the campus. The air was filled with the fragrance of spring, and only faint voices of children could be heard. They were happy voices, sweetened by all the unlearned lessons of the world.

My walk took me past the administration building. In the lighted window I could see Mrs. Sloop at her desk. I went in to sit one last time in front of her. She leaned back in her chair, smiled and said, "Well, Anne, you must be excited about going to Washington."

We reminisced about my early days at Crossnore, went over some last-minute correspondence that had been part of my job for two years, and then we said our farewells.

"We will see each other again, my dear," she told me. "For all of us who have lived here, the absence is not for long. These hills will call to you, and you will return," she said with the wisdom of one who had seen generations of children leave her school.

We embraced, she gave me a small photograph of herself, and we said goodnight.

Dottie and I put off our parting until just before we boarded our separate buses to go home. One of Dottie's greatest gifts was disguising her emotions with laughter. She interpreted life by standing on the outside and looking in—finding some humor in the behavior of people. But tears rolled down her dimpled cheeks as we clung together. That was the last time I saw Dottie, but I will not forget her.

———————

Going home was different now. Daddy had returned from the Army, and he and Mother had built their dream house. A long circular drive led up to the house, which faced a small, clear lake. There was a serenity about the setting, with the woods all around and white ducks and brown mallards gliding peacefully across the lake. Birds came to nest in the bird houses, Mother had more room for her flowers, and Daddy had a large vegetable garden.

Daddy had built his own hardware store in town, and establishing business had been easy for him. His friendly manner, his interest in people, and his honesty won him hundreds of regular customers. If someone was having trouble with a lawnmower, Daddy would fix it at no charge. If a customer came in and Daddy wasn't busy, they might play a game of checkers and talk. At the front of the store was a candy counter, and neighborhood children came into the store for candy and a bit of Daddy's teasing.

When I arrived at the Charlotte station from Crossnore, Mother and Lynda were there to meet me. Lynda was a tall, leggy ten-year-old. I had missed most of her growing up years, but after she had started school, she often included notes and drawings in Mother's letters to me. When I went home for summers and holidays, I played games with her and took her to the movies. Seeing her run to meet me, I regretted having already missed so much of her life, knowing that she would grow up while I was away in Washington.

Mother watched me come toward her. I was now three inches taller than she, and as I bent down to kiss her cheek, she said, "You did it, Anne—I knew you could."

Two days later she stood with me again on that platform in Charlotte, waiting for the train that would take me to Washington. Beside me was my new green suitcase, packed with clothes and toiletries befitting a young lady about to begin her first job.

Mother looked at the suitcase for a long, reflecting moment. "Do you like it, Anne?" she asked.

"Oh, yes," I answered, "very much."

"You won't clutter it with sticky candy and old walnuts, will you?"

"Never," I said, as we hugged each other and laughed.

I had said goodbye to Carolyn, Marilynn, and Lynda that morning. Carolyn had finished high school the year before and chose not to go to college. She had an excellent job as a secretary and was happy with her independence. Marilynn was thirteen. We had spent the summer before together, singing duets while she played the piano, the two of us rowing to the other side of the lake to look for snakes, and taking long walks. She took my departure with her usual flippancy, but we both knew how much we would miss each other.

Betty, twenty-two, had graduated from high school a year early because she was so smart. She had finished college and was a medical technologist at a hospital in

South Carolina. In her final year at college she was chosen May Queen, and was runner-up in the Miss South Carolina pageant. Mother and Daddy were very proud of her.

On that June morning in 1950, Mother and I stood on the platform talking about all the wrong things. Wasn't it hot for late spring? Did I like the color of my new dress? Would I write often? Then the conductor called, "All aboard," and Mother and I walked to the door of the train. What I wanted to say was suddenly lost as I looked down at her—how small and vulnerable she was. I wanted to apologize for the hours of worry I had caused, but there was no time. She held me close for a moment, and then she said, "I want you to enjoy life, Anne, but always be a lady."

We waved to each other until her tiny figure disappeared in the billowing steam. As the train headed north to Washington, I realized for the first time how complete was my love for the Nyes. They had not felt sorry for me because I was an orphan dressed in shabby clothes; from the beginning, they had set about fashioning me into a worthy person.

Mother—with her shy manners, her strong sense of what is correct, and her ability to understand the needs of my sisters and me—had managed to unravel my fears and cares. Daddy, who greeted life with an open smile and a handshake, had taught me how to row a boat and bait a fishhook. He may have preferred comics to the classics, but he had filled the great void left by my real father.

I settled back in my seat on the train, ready to begin life on my own.

It had been arranged through Mrs. Sloop that I live with a family in Washington, and I quickly became a part of that family. Mr. Rossman—I called him Papa—was a tall, heavyset man in his sixties, full of good humor and tricks. He offered to instruct me in the game of golf; I ended up being the caddy. He saw to it that I never lacked for mail; all the letters marked "occupant" he carefully readdressed to me. We developed a great liking for each other.

Mrs. Rossman—who became Mama to me—was small, fluttery, and very concerned about my welfare. She loved to keep house, shop, and prepare elaborate Sunday dinners. Her only daughter was away at school, and in a way I guess I took her place.

Although Papa was a prosperous and respected bank examiner, they were very unpretentious people, living in a small frame house in northwest Washington. He drove an old Buick sedan from about 1940. He knew all the streets and hills in that part of the city and just which ones his car could navigate. Riding with him was an experience.

After my sheltered life in the mountains, Washington was a challenge. But I faced it head on. After six months I became secretary to the director of a large government agency. I took lessons at the YWCA in golf, tennis, and bridge, and spent my spare time in the museums and art galleries and in finding my way around the city.

In my second year in Washington, I met Richard, a writer-photographer for the Department of State. I was intrigued by his wit, good manners, and adventurous nature. After a game of tennis, we might sit by the Potomac reading Shakespeare or Pogo. We once started out to a movie and ended up in Philadelphia. On another occasion we drove to Rising Sun, Maryland to watch the sun come up.

His assignments for the State Department had taken him all over the United States. Sometimes on an assignment in Washington, he took me along as "caption writer." I helped Richard cover President Eisenhower's inauguration, and that evening we had passes to the inaugural balls. The pictures and stories Richard would do from these assignments became part of the publications that the State Department distributed to foreign countries. It was an exciting adventure.

I knew from the beginning Richard was not ordinary. His knowledge was, for me, like looking into a deep well, and his wit could send me into uncontrollable laughter. He was gentle, kind, and attentive.

I went home for holidays and found Mother always eager to hear about my life in Washington. She would sit in the rocking chair in her room, and I would lie across her bed, relating my adventures. One weekend I took Richard home with me. There was immediate rapport between Mother and him, and when I left to return to Washington, she said, "Marry him."

On a bright crisp day in October, 1953, Richard and I were married in a little church in northwest Washington. Mother came up to supervise the preparations and to stand proudly beside me at the reception. All my sisters were bridesmaids, and Papa Rossman gave me away.

Four years later we had a son, naming him Richard for his father and calling him Dickie. When he was a year old, we took him to Charlotte for a visit, and Mother treated him in a doting grandmotherly way. The first evening we were there, Daddy came in with a little brown bag. "Guess what Granddaddy has for you," he said, with that look in his eye I had seen many years before.

In the bag were lollipops for Dickie, just as there had been for me. For a moment I remembered a frightened little girl who bore marks of betrayal, shyly accepting her first bag of candy from this sandy-haired man.

I smiled at the memory, for this man was now my Daddy and my feeling for him went beyond gratitude.

On my trips home, I often walked with Daddy to his garden to gather tomatoes, and sometimes we sat by the lake just talking. He was never one to meddle, but if I had a problem, he was a good listener. He had taught us to be optimistic, saying, "If it doesn't work today, then make it work tomorrow."

On one of those visits, I asked Daddy, "Whatever happened to the woman in black who brought us to you and Mother?" This was a question I had long been afraid to ask, but now I felt the need to know.

For a moment he seemed startled that I remembered that day so long ago. Then quietly he said, "Well, Anne, she just never came back for you and your sisters."

"Why did you keep us, Daddy?" I asked.

"Because we loved you too much to let you go," he said, looking past me at his recollection of that time.

In the summer of 1959, I received my first and only telephone call from Aunt Carrie. "Your father died this morning, Anne," she said in a sorrowing voice.

"I am sorry to hear that," was all I could reply.

"It would be nice if you, Betty, and Carolyn could come to the funeral," she continued. "Your father has no other relatives."

My sisters and I had often wondered about our father. We had received only two short notes after he had remarried, both from his new wife. One was to tell us they had a son, the other announced the birth of a daughter. We had taken the news with indifference, not realizing that we now had a half-brother and a half-sister.

I was silent throughout the long drive from Washington to Charlotte, my head awhirl with questions. Who was this man who needed me to mourn him? What had taken him back to North Carolina? Why did I feel so little emotion?

There were intermittent flashes of the man who had given me love and laughter, and I tried to hold those moments in my mind. But they clouded over and would not stay. Instead I saw Carolyn's tear-stained face and heard her asking, "Will our daddy come for us today?" I saw Betty that wintry day at the Coburns'—the wind whipping through her thin coat—as she shouted, "Run, Anne!" to save me from Benny with the pitchfork.

I felt again the sting of abuse, and my striking out at playmates when it was something else I hated. And there were many voices that I felt rather than heard, saying, "Put your things in your suitcases, girls, you are leaving here today." The fear, humiliation, and helplessness of those years as orphans swept over me once more.

I wanted now to find a way and a reason to say farewell to my father, and I found it in what Mother had told me years earlier. "He is your father, Anne, and you must love and respect him for that, if nothing more."

No other relatives, Aunt Carrie had said. How strange. All these years I had assumed that my father had been living in New York with his wife and their two children.

When I arrived in Charlotte, Betty told me that things had not gone well for our father and his wife, and that they had separated. He had apparently returned to Charlotte—when, we never learned—but made no attempt to join whatever relatives he had there. We think now he had forgotten that once he had three daughters.

Aunt Carrie showed us a clipping from a Charlotte newspaper of two years before. "Pauper Poet Seeks Reason for Being in Works of Robert Burns." There was a picture of my father, and I studied it until it is imprinted in my mind even today.

The wavy white hair was covered by a battered old hat, and the eyes that had been blue as the sea were now heavy with age and disappointment. A large-framed man, the story said, who had lost a leg in an automobile accident. A man troubled by the state of the world and his inability to exist in it, except at the county home. A pauper poet, who wrote and recited poetry.

His favorite verses, he had told the reporter, Charles Kuralt, were those of Robert Burns and the Bible. "I prefer David the Psalmist. Perhaps you remember . . . 'Weeping may endure for a night, but joy cometh in the morning.'

"And there is always Bobby Burns . . . 'Man's inhumanity to man makes countless thousands mourn.' "

Then my heart turned over. My father had recited for the reporter the first few lines of "Little Boy Blue":

"Time was when the little toy dog was new, and the soldier passing fair;

"And that was the time when our Little Boy Blue, had kissed them and put them there."

That was a poem from our childhood. Why did he include this with Robert Burns and the Bible? Talking there with Charles Kuralt, did my father recall that a quarter-century ago he had recited those verses, perhaps to three little girls? I could not ask him, now or ever. I would never know.

Seeing those words on the newspaper page, my father's picture beside them, I could hear his voice putting all the inflections in the right places, as he gestured with his hands. How strange that his love of poetry had endured through all those years. Perhaps it was all that had remained for him. Could it be that, in his own way, he had suffered as much as I? It was then I wept, not only for his death but for his wasted life.

Mother went with us to the funeral, a simple service held at the funeral home chapel. I do not recall the eulogy. I remember only the soft strains of the organ, the tears in Mother's eyes as she sat with Betty, Carolyn and me, and my bitterness turning to sorrow.

After the service, she invited our relatives to come home with us. My aunts had not met Mrs. Nye, and I sensed their disapproval when I introduced her as "my mother."

Aunt Thelma was there. Her hair was white, her face had remained beautiful. She seemed happy to see my sisters and me and chatted about her family. Aunt Anne's face was passive and drawn, her small thin hands trembled as she took my own and studied my face. Her husband had died some years before, she had no children, and now she was alone. I felt a brief surge of pity for this frail, lonely woman.

Aunt Carrie was also there. We had kept in touch with her, however, through Christmas cards and occasional visits to the shop in Charlotte where she worked. But the subject of our orphan life was always carefully ignored.

The mountains of the Blue Ridge did beckon, as Mrs. Sloop had said they would, and one summer I returned. The gravel crunched under the car wheels as my husband and I made our way up the mountain to the Crossnore campus. I heard the familiar sound of the looms in the weaving room. I saw Mr. Obie coming out of the dining room, as I had seen him do so many times before.

I found Mrs. Sloop in the administration building, sitting at her desk as though she had not moved since my graduation night. She walked with some difficulty now, but the light in her eyes had not dimmed. There was still a magic in her touch, and I smiled at the memories I had of this determined woman who had helped me find my way.

She told me of Dr. Sloop's death the year before, and of the chapel that had been built on the campus in his memory. She told me of plans for new dormitories, and of Crossnore children who had graduated and done well in the world. The years had not dimmed her ambitions for the school or for her children.

Except for the new chapel, Crossnore was just as I had left it. How untouched and protected it seemed. I wanted to tell the people here about the world beyond these hills. There is so much they do not know, I thought.

Then the chapel carillon began to chime. I watched the late-afternoon sun send streaks of light through the trees, to fall softly on the village nestled in the mountains so close to the sky. I felt a quiet peace and a new love for the mountains and these gentle people, and I realized that it was I who lacked knowledge.

With my husband I walked across the campus, wanting to recapture the spirit of this place that was so far from the hostilities of life. It was not quite dark when we reached the lake where the children from the school ice skated in winter. I crossed the small wooden bridge, and saw again the rock where I had sat as a young girl with a new green suitcase, where I had shed my grief for what once was and learned to accept what is.

My sisters and I had agreed to have a family gathering in Charlotte for Thanksgiving, 1962. It wasn't often that we all got together, and Mother and Daddy were excited at having us home. Betty was married, had three sons, and lived in South Carolina. Carolyn, also married, was in Pittsburgh. Marilynn lived in California with her husband

and four children, and Lynda had one more year at the University. We could all be there except Marilynn.

As my husband turned the car into the long, curving drive, I saw Mother standing near the house, her arms laden with pine cones for decorating. I saw Daddy down by the lake, wearing his baseball cap and feeding the ducks. They were gathered about him making noises, and I knew he was talking to them.

I had truly seen kings and queens, I had met with the elite, I had danced at the White House. But all those triumphs paled at the sight of my mother and father, waving to welcome me home. My heart was filled with thanksgiving for these two people, who had taken my life of nothing and made it into everything.

———————

Mother died the following summer.

———————

Going back to Charlotte for her funeral was, I think, the saddest day of my life. I could not believe she would not be there to hear the stories I had saved up to tell her. I had read a book she would have liked, we had taken a trip she would have enjoyed hearing about, my garden was in full summer bloom.

She had always been so happy when her children came to visit. There were special treats for the grandchildren. Meals were served on her best china. We would stay up—my sisters, Mother and I—talking far into the night. Now we would be there but she would not.

The service was in the church where my sisters and I had been baptized, where we had attended Sunday school as children. The choir soloist sang "Swing Low, Sweet Chariot" in a clear soprano, but it was Mother's voice I heard from twenty years before, comforting us through the dark nights of 1942. "Her children shall rise and call her Blessed," said the minister, and I heard no more. My grief closed around me, and I withdrew into my memories.

Returning home after the service, I did not go into the house. Instead I walked down to the lake and sat alone on the bench, where I had so many times sat with Mother as we snapped beans from the garden.

The world slowly darkened. Strange grey shadows lay all around me. There were no clouds—it was an eclipse of the sun. I hated it and shivered in the faded half-light.

Then suddenly the shadows were gone and the sun broke through, like the crescendo of a great orchestra. The pine trees and sky again were mirrored in the lake. Lost for a moment in the reality that Mother was gone, I was unaware that Daddy was standing beside me.

I stood up and we walked together toward the house. "I miss her already, Daddy," I said.

"So do I," he replied, his voice choking.

As we neared the house, we came to one of her gardens. Red primrose and yellow daisies were reaching to the sun. Would they wither now without Mother's care? I wondered. No, I smiled. She would have made certain that their roots were deep, and they would come up year after year without her.

Leaning against a tree was the hoe she had used a few days before. I wanted to see her there, wearing her big straw hat and humming a Stephen Foster song. I wanted once more to see her shy half-smile.

Daddy moved quietly away as I put my face in my hands and cried. Filled with an overwhelming sense of loss, I thought—I can't live without you, Mother.

"Never say I can't," came her voice, echoing through my mind.

EPILOGUE

We seldom go back to Charlotte anymore. There is little there for me now but memories.

Daddy—we call him Granddaddy now because of our boys—sold his house with its lakes and mallard ducks when he moved down to Lumberton in 1978.

My two sisters live in Atlanta with their families, and Betty, ever the leader, is already a grandmother. Lynda and her family are in Winston-Salem. Marilynn is back in Charlotte from California, and has a small house within sight of our old home. From her kitchen window she can almost see the lake where she and I went rowing.

We all made one last visit to Granddaddy's house just before it was to be sold. We wanted to sort through closets and cabinets for things that should be saved. I came across a small silver plaque on a walnut base, carefully wrapped, in the back of a dresser drawer. On it were engraved the words "To Our Mother of All the Years," with names of her five girls.

I remembered it well. I had nominated Mother to be North Carolina Mother of the Year for 1962, and had sent in the forms, endorsements, and all the rest to state headquarters in Raleigh. It was obvious to me why she should be named, and should be apparent to anyone.

It was not to be. The State Mother that year was a deserving woman who had combined politics, family, and a career. But Mrs. Nye—my mother—was first alternate, and she did go to Raleigh for the ceremonies, was interviewed and photographed and made much of, and came back to Charlotte a celebrity. My husband then had the plaque made up, and we sent it to her as our mother of all the years.

Daddy later told me it was just as well she had not been named State Mother. "She is in failing health, you know, and she could not have taken all that travel and attention."

It was then I realized that she had not long to live, and I was glad I had not waited to tell her of my love and respect.

———————

One of our joys, I have said, were the walks my sisters and I would take with our father. On one such walk—the last, I think, that we made—we stopped in Woolworth's to have our pictures made in one of those little booths. I remember treasuring those photos when I was six, but like most of our belongings they were left behind when the woman in black first took us away.

In the 1960s—after my father's death—a small package arrived at my home in Washington. In it were those photos and other family pictures, apparently kept by one of our aunts for more than twenty years.

I am looking at those photos as I write this. Betty, age seven, is in the middle of a small, three-section frame. She is blond, blue eyed and smiling at the world. Carolyn is on the right, not yet five, with dark eyes and auburn curls, an Italian Madonna. I look defiantly from the left frame, coming up on age six and already stubborn in attitude and appearance.

In a larger, separate frame is the photo of my father, made on that same last walk. He is unsmiling but not unfriendly, a physically big man, and even bigger then to his little girls.

The dime-store photo and the story by Charles Kuralt are all that we have of him. The rest is memory.

Part of that memory I have kept by naming our second son Timothy Malcolm—Timothy because it becomes him, and Malcolm for my father.

The orphanage is gone now, I am told. It was razed ten years ago and the grounds made into a little park. But the chapel still stands under the willow oaks, maintained by the City of Charlotte as an historical landmark. I am glad that some part of it was kept, because I know now that—for all its uncertainty—an orphanage can be a happy place for a child.

Somewhere north of Charlotte will be the Stamens' farm, where Bucky taught me to fight and to win at marbles. I shall not go looking for it, because I did not know then where we were and would not know now. Nor shall I go looking for the Coburn place. That was an experience no child should have to recall.

But I will return to Crossnore, because I sense that there, in those gentle mountains, I yielded the last grief and anger of that girl long ago whose father never came back to claim her.

"Children toss'd to and fro," says Ephesians. Children betrayed, I would add, speaking for the child I was then and for foster children of today.

We were reclaimed from the Stamens' only when our illness alarmed Mrs. Stamens. We were rescued from the Coburn's only when Benny's violence threatened our lives. And we stayed on at the Nye's—sent there for a week at most—because the social worker never came back for us. They kept us because they loved us.

This is too haphazard a way to handle the lives of children. We survived, but not all do.

———————

The Mecklenburg county clerk has said that they have records that would tell me more about my father, my sisters, and myself. I am not sure that I want to know.

What if I find that an aunt or uncle arranged to have us taken from our father, but instead of taking us into their homes, had us made wards of the state? What if I find that our father signed away all rights to us—knowingly or not—and then forgot about us? I may prefer to live with a story that I have come to know and understand.

I may not ask the county clerk to see the records on us. My ties with that part of my past are fragile, and it may be that my memory of those times is all I need.

Anne Hall Whitt
May 1982

ABOUT THE AUTHOR

Raising her two sons has been Anne Hall Whitt's first concern, but now that they are grown, she can disappear in to the gardening and needlework she loves. She can also speak out, as she does in *The Suitcases* and will do in other writings, on the injustices done to children. The author lives with her husband and two sons in Gaithersburg, Maryland.

Studies in Sociology from MENTOR and SIGNET CLASSIC

(0451)

☐ **THE PLEASURES OF SOCIOLOGY edited by Lewis A. Coser.** Sociology comes alive in this collection of thirty-six of the clearest, most stimulating writings in the field. With a combination of deep insight and excellent literary style, some of the greatest sociological thinkers come to grips with the most enduring questions about the individual and society. Introduction by the editor. With a list of suggested additional readings. (622642—$4.50)*

☐ **URBAN LEGACY: The Story of America's Cities by Diana Klebanow, Franklin L. Jonas and Ira M. Leonard.** A vivid history of American cities from colonial times to the '70s. *Urban Legacy* traces the progressive urbanization and suburbanization of American society and the impact of urbanism upon American life, including unemployment, the flight to the suburbs, bankruptcy and crime. Illustrations. Maps. Bibliography. Political Cartoons.

(615867—$2.95)

☐ **A WELFARE MOTHER by Susan Sheehan.** The profile of a New York City welfare mother: her life with various "husbands" and her nine children. A moving account of the culture of poverty. "This is life on its own terms . . . a fine achievement, a perfect book . . . should be read!"—*Saturday Review.* Winner of a Sidney Hillman award for innovative reporting on a social problem. Introduction by Michael Harrington. (619498—$2.25)

☐ **TWENTY YEARS AT HULL HOUSE by Jane Addams.** Foreword by Henry Steele Commager. A graphic account of the famed Chicago settlement house from 1889–1909. Bibliography, Biographical Note, drawings, index and photographs included. (515641—$2.50)

*Price slightly higher in Canada

Buy them at your local bookstore or use this convenient coupon for ordering.

THE NEW AMERICAN LIBRARY, INC.,
P.O. Box 999, Bergenfield, New Jersey 07621

Please send me the books I have checked above. I am enclosing $_____
(please add $1.00 to this order to cover postage and handling). Send check or money order—no cash or C.O.D.'s. Prices and numbers are subject to change without notice.

Name_____

Address_____

City _____ State _____ Zip Code _____

Allow 4-6 weeks for delivery.

This offer is subject to withdrawal without notice.